The Scrapbooker's Guide to Business
What You Need to Know
Before You Invest

by
Kathy Steligo

Second Edition, Revised

Carlo Press
San Carlos, California

D1501525

Published by:

Carlo Press, PO Box 7019, San Carlos, CA 94070
Tel: 800-431-1579
fax: 650-592-3790
website: www.carlopress.com
e-mail: carlop@pacbell.net

This publication is designed to provide accurate information in regard to the subject matter covered. It is sold with the understanding that the publisher is not engaged in rendering legal or other professional services.

Front cover and section page credits: Graphic images are copyright and courtesy of me & my BIG ideas.

Copyright © 2000, 2002 by Kathy Steligo
Second Printing 2002, revised

PRINTED IN THE USA

10 9 8 7 6 5 4 3 2

Publisher's Cataloging in Publication Data:

Steligo, Kathy
    The scrapbooker's guide to business : what you need to know
    before you invest / Kathy Steligo.
    160 p. : ill. ; .8128 cm.
    Includes index.
    ISBN 0-9669799-2-3 (pbk.)
    1. New Business Enterprises. 2. Home-based Business.
    3. Self-employment. 4. Scrapbooks.
  658'.041--dc20   00-104972

DEDICATION

To scrappers everywhere who dream of getting paid for doing something they love—and then make it happen.

ACKNOWLEDGMENTS

Thank you to all the scrapreneurs who took the time to share their ideas and experiences. A very special thanks to Stephanie Rahmatulla for generously sharing her wonderful "little people" for the book's cover and section pages.

What others are saying about this book:

"Just the book for scrappers interested in starting their own business."
— *Creating Keepsakes* Magazine

"Steligo walks you through the process of starting the type of scrapbook business that is right for you." — *Memory Makers* Magazine

"An excellent source of information for the prospective, new, or experienced scrapbook business owner. Wonderful tips and guidelines." — Dane Ann Clark, The Scrapbook Connection

"If you ever thought about making money in scrapbooking (part or full-time), Steligo's tips will definitely make it easier." — Caroline Meisel, My Memories

"Steligo has done all the research for you." — Victoria Walker, The Scrapbook Corner

"Provides an excellent overview of the business opportunities related to the craft of scrapbooking...multiple examples in various categories!" — K.H., Phoenix, AZ

"Your book is wonderful!" — K.M. from Annapolis, MD

"Lots of ideas I hadn't thought of." — L.S. from Owosso, MI

"Well written and easy to read." — DK from San Diego, CA

"This book inspired me! If other people can make a success of planning retreats, so can I. Thanks for the push to get started." — S.B. from Shelby, NC

Contents

PART III: Understanding Business Basics

INTRODUCTION

Fueled by the innovation and commitment of people who love the craft, the scrapbooking industry is exploding with growth and shows no signs of stopping. In 2001, sales of scrapbooking materials, supplies and other related items amounted to $1.4 billion year. Not bad for a hobby that was "reborn" just a few short years ago. New businesses, techniques, and products appear with incredible frequency, much to the delight of the 26 million U.S. households (and many others around the world) where scrapbooking is a regular pastime; or, as many of us refer to it—an obsession.

More and more scrappers—those who have been bitten, and are now smitten with the scrapbooking bug—are scurrying to become "scrapreneurs," by turning their passion into profits. Many succeed and steadily grow their businesses, while others quit or fail because they choose the wrong business, lack required skills, or are simply unprepared for what it takes to run a business successfully. Whether you're ready to invest a few dollars and a few hours, or give your business everything you've got, YOU CAN SUCCEED if you plan well. That's what this book offers you: a look at what you need to know and consider *before* you invest your time and money.

How This Book Will Help You

This book will help you broaden your thinking, consider different possibilities, and get a glimpse into specific business opportunities. Along the way, you'll find ideas, tips, resources, and expertise from current scrapbook business owners. Here's what you'll find inside:

Part I: Bringing Your Dream into Focus will help you define your motivation, skills, and goals. These introductory steps lay the foundation for choosing the business that best matches the investment and commitment you're willing to make.

Part II: Finding the Right Business for You describes nine different ways to make money from scrapbooking. You might decide to focus on one business, (perhaps a retail or Internet store) or combine several (maybe you want to have a home store, sponsor crops, and teach workshops). Whatever your motivation, read through each chapter, because the ideas and resources mentioned in one chapter may apply to others. Because initial investment and potential profit differ greatly depending on many variables, each business is ranked as "low," "moderate," or "high," regarding start-up cost, income potential, commitment, and financial risk.

Part III: Understanding Business Basics: This information will be helpful no matter what scrapbooking business you select. You'll find answers to common questions like, "do I need a license?" "how do I register my business name?" and "how much should I charge?" Get tips about figuring start-up costs, accepting credit card payments, promoting your business, choosing a partner, and much more.

Each chapter is introduced with a unique icon. Where the icon appears in the chapter text, you'll find an idea, suggestion, or tip. Two other icons appear throughout the book:

Information from existing scrapbook business owners.

Survey Says! features results from The National Scrapbook Survey conducted in May 2000. These results reflect responses of 52 retail store owners and 229 scrapbook consultants.

Whatever business you choose, I wish you good luck, lots of fun, and much success!

Kathy Steligo

Part I:
Bringing Your
Dream Into Focus

⊙   The Path To Success

⊙   Know What You Really Want

⊙   Do You Have What It Takes?

Whatever you can do or dream you can, begin it. Boldness has genius, magic, and power in it. Begin it now.—Goethe

Chapter 1.
The Path To Success

Few things in life are more satisfying than getting paid for doing something you love. Many scrappers are finding they can do just that. If you're one of the millions who enjoy a scrapbooking obsession, you can profit from your passion in a way that fits into your schedule and lifestyle.

Opportunities for Scrapreneurs

The growing scrapbook industry continues to create new opportunities for profit. These business opportunities fall into three distinct categories:

Retail. Selling scrapbook products and services directly to customers from your store, your website, or your home. Your profit is made directly from consumers.

Wholesale. You sell products (usually your own) at a discount to scrapbook suppliers, who then increase the price and resell to consumers. Your profit is made from other businesses.

Service. You offer a service, rather than a product. Your profit is made from consumers or other businesses.

Whether you want to make $100 or $10,000 a month, there are many scrap-booking business options available. The real question is which business offers the best match for your personality, skills, desired level of commitment and goals. You'll learn more about potential scrapbooking businesses in Part II. First, let's focus on what you should consider before you choose a business.

Look Before You Leap

Why do more than 50% of small business ventures fail? One reason, according to the Small Business Administration (SBA), is because so many entrepreneurs simply don't know how to run a business. A plumber may know how to fix leaky sinks, but not about marketing or balancing the books. A hairdresser's skill with a pair of scissors and a blow dryer doesn't prepare her to keep her business afloat. It's the same with scrapbooking. Enthusiasm and technical skills are important for your business, but they're just not enough.Not that there's anything wrong with enthusiasm—it's wonderful. In fact, it's a requirement for success. But to succeed you need to know your craft *and* have business skills as well.

It's so exciting to think of having your own scrapbook business! You lie awake at night thinking how you'll stock your shelves. You scribble a mountain of little notes to yourself at every opportunity. You just can't wait to design your busi-ness card or outline all the workshops you plan to teach. You find yourself doodling new logos as you chat on the telephone or watch television.

You *can* be successful. But resist the temptation to plunge into the business world before you're adequately prepared. It's wiser to first channel all that wonderful motivation into careful research and thorough planning. Consider what you really want from your business, both personally and professionally, and what it will take to get there. Invest time before you invest money. You'll be firmly on the path to success: better prepared and more likely to meet your goals.

The Path to Success

How do you transform a great idea into a successful business? How much start-up money will you need? How much money can you make?

Do you need a business license? How do you find customers? So many questions! Your pre-business planning should find answers to all these questions, and more.

Which of the following examples seems more logical?

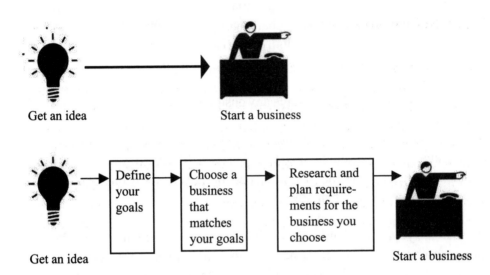

Get an idea   Start a business

Get an idea   Start a business

Starting your business as shown in the first example is like shooting at a target with your eyes closed: you may score a hit if you're lucky, but the odds are against you. Taking careful aim on business requirements, as the second example shows, greatly improves your likelihood of scoring a professional bullseye.

Convert Your Fears into Confidence

If you're like many people, the thought of starting your own business is both exciting and terrifying. You have doubts about your abilities, you don't know where to begin, and you hate the thought of putting your investment at risk. If you're used to working for someone else, maybe the idea of making all your own decisions, or giving up a secure income and benefits is scary. Perhaps you dread the potential embarrassment and disappointment of possible failure. The good news is, you're normal!

Understandably, many people have the same misgivings about starting a business. It's better to be cautious than overconfident. Don't let your fears scare you away. Instead, use them to motivate you to find out more about the business you want to pursue. Banish anxieties with research and planning.

You can't foresee for every mishap that may occur, but you can acquire the confidence and ability to deal with challenges you encounter along the way. You can face your fears head on with a Fear List that includes every trepidation you have about starting your business. Here's an example:

My fear: I'm afraid I won't have any customers.

My action: I'll learn how to promote my business by reading books, checking Internet resources, and taking classes. I'll carefully define my target market, and create a solid marketing plan before I start my business. I'll also ask other retailers for their advice.

Now create your own Fear List. Candidly explore what you fear most about pursuing a business. Then describe the actions that will eliminate, or at least control, each fear. Include any of the following sample issues if they apply to you, then add others that concern you. As you continue through this book, and during your business planning, develop action steps to address each of your fears.

Business Fear List

I'm afraid: Action steps:
I'll be overwhelmed.
I'll have too much responsibility.
Customers won't like my work.
There's too much competition.
I won't make enough money.
I won't meet my loan payments.
I won't have time for my family.
I won't know where to go for help.

_____

_____

_____

Later, when you've completed all the action steps, review your Fear List again. If any item still gives you goosebumps, identify additional action steps until you feel more confident.

You're going to hit bumps as you travel the road to success. Addressing your fears and preparing adequately for your business will help you fly right over them...or at least find a way around them.

Five Ways to Find Time to Plan Your Business

1. Get up earlier or go to bed later (even one hour can help).

2. Use your lunch break.

3. Give up TV one or two nights a week.

4. Consolidate the time you spend doing errands and chores.

5. Ask the family to take on more responsibility around the house to give you some extra time.

Find something you love to do, then find a way to get paid to do it.
—Anonymous

 Chapter 2.
Know What You Really Want

As you'll discover in Part II, there are many different ways to profit from scrapbooking. The method you choose depends on your personal, financial, and business goals; the skills and knowledge required; and just how much time, money, and effort you're willing to invest.

Know Thyself!

First, you need to know what you want, and, just as importantly, what you don't want. This may sound simplistic, but choosing a business before you define what you want is putting the cart before the horse.

Operating a retail store may be a good choice if you're willing to invest thousands of dollars and work 50-60 hours a week. If you prefer to simplify your life or spend more time with your family, starting a home store or consultant business may be a better choice for you. If your preference is to spend a few hours each week actually working on scrapbooks, consider creating albums for others.

Maybe you have a mind for details and thrive on multi-tasking. In that case, coordinating swaps, crops, getaways, or other scrapbooking events may be just your cup of tea.

Why bother with all this soul searching? Because you're more likely to succeed—and have fun doing it—if you choose a business that supports, rather than conflicts, with your personal priorities.

Define Your Goals

A '60s era poster advised, "If you don't know where you're going, you can't get there!" That's true in your professional, as well as your personal life. It makes sense to first define what you want, then decide which scrapbooking business can get you there without too many detours.

Perhaps you're ready for a lifestyle change. Possibly you're a stay-at-home-mom who wants to make enough income to pay for the annual family vacation. Maybe your kids just left the nest, you've recently retired, or you've suddenly found yourself unemployed. Or, like many scrappers, you may simply be looking for a way to pay for your growing scrapbooking habit.

Whatever your motivation, identify your priorities before you begin your business. Start by making two columns on a piece of paper. Label the first column "Personal Goals." Begin listing your goals, including those concerning scrapbooking, yourself, and your family. Using the list below, delete goals that don't apply, and add any of your own.

Don't rush through this exercise. Take the time to be thoughtful, realistic, and thorough. Be as specific as you can: "I want to make at least $15,000 a year" is more helpful than "I want to make a lot of money."

> **Personal Goals**
> Spend more time with my family/kids
> Spend more time scrapbooking
> Expand my scrapbooking skills
> Experience less stress
> Have weekends off
> Learn to speak French
> Meet new people, make new friends
> Become more involved in my community
> Go back to school and complete my degree
> Other (describe other personal goals)

Once your list is complete, go back and prioritize your goals, listing the most important first, then the next important, and so on.

In the second column, list your specific business goals, adding your own to any of the following that apply:

Business Goals
Be successful
Be my own boss
Not have to deal with employees
Work part-time
Own the biggest scrapbooking store in the country
Make enough to pay my home mortgage
Work no more than 30 hours a week
Other (describe your other primary business goals)

Now prioritize your business goals as you did with your personal goals. Let both lists "rest" for a few days, then review them and make any changes you wish. Compare the two lists to see if any of your business goals conflict with your personal goals. For example, "owning the biggest store in the country" conflicts with most of the personal goals. If you plan to go to school and complete your degree, a part-time business that doesn't conflict with homework and classtime is a better choice than a business that demands your full-time attention.

If you have conflicting goals, you need to make some important decisions. Then adjust one list or the other until both lists are compatible. Use your completed list of defined goals to choose the right scrapbooking business for you. Stay enthusiastic and focused by frequently reviewing your goals.

A Surprising Motivation?

According to a survey by the National Federation of Small Business Owners, profit motivated less than 20% of those surveyed to start their businesses. Most said they wanted to be their own boss.

Obstacles don't have to stop you. If you run into a wall, don't turn around and give up. Figure out how to climb it, go through it, or work around it.
—Michael Jordan

Chapter 3.
Do You Have What It Takes?

Now that you've identified your personal and business goals, it's time to evaluate whether you have what it takes to operate a business successfully. Simply stated, to achieve business success, you need:

Passion + Knowledge + Skills

Of course, you'll also need time, energy, commitment, and cash to start your business and keep it going. But if you have the passion to stay motivated, the knowledge to succeed, and the skill to implement what you know, you will be successful.

The Power of Passion

Nothing propels a relationship or a business more successfully than passion. Romantic passion fuels creativity, sees you through tough times, and sustains the longterm commitment necessary to attain your goals. Professional passion can do the same for your business. When you're in love, you're happy to overlook the little things that would otherwise annoy you. Passion brings that same essential motivation to your business. All the passion in the world can't replace the people and business skills you need to succeed, but a business started without passion won't be around for long. Business superstars—Bill Gates, Donald Trump, or Lisa Bearnson of *Creating Keepsakes*—have intense enthusiasm for what they do. Their unrelenting devotion to their businesses motivates their continuing success.

So, what exactly are *your* intentions? Is your interest in scrapbooking an infatuation or a passing fancy? If so, maybe a business in a different industry is a better choice for you. On the other hand, if your closets, drawers, and dining room table are overflowing with papers, punches, borders, and stickers, and you prefer to spend every free minute scrapping, forge on. You have all the symptoms of being head-over-heels smitten. Use that passion to drive your business ideas.

Knowledge is Power

Knowledge is information you possess. Regardless of the business you choose, you'll need both scrapbooking and business knowledge. Once you get your license and hang out your shingle, you're not in Kansas anymore —you've crossed the threshold from beloved hobby to bonafide business. Then it's time to put what you've learned into action.

You'll need to be well-informed about various scrapbooking products, tools, terminology, and techniques. You'll also need to be particularly knowledgeable, if not expert, regarding the specific type of business you choose. If you want to teach rubber stamping classes, you must be more knowledgeable about different types of stamps, inks, and techniques than if you plan to sell rubber stamps from your Internet or home store.

Why Businesses Fail

According to a Dun & Bradstreet study, 90% of all small business failures are due to poor management resulting from lack of knowledge.

Skills: Learn by Doing

Skill is the ability to apply your knowledge to accomplish something. While knowledge is something you learn or have instinctively, a skill is acquired by experience. Watching someone create album pages over and over doesn't give you the same skill.

It may provide the knowledge of how to do it, but you don't become skilled until you complete several pages yourself. Would you want to buy a car from a salesman who didn't know how to drive or have the information to close the sale?

When it comes to your business, consider both the general and specific skills required. Ideally, your business should involve what you do best and enjoy the most. If you're a great scrapper but hate getting up in front of people, pick something other than teaching (or realize you need to overcome your reluctance).

Students won't be satisfied with your class on pocket pages if you can't adequately demonstrate or explain how to create one. Nor will they be very enthusiastic about taking another of your classes or encouraging others do so.

Once you identify the knowledge and skills you need for the business you've chosen (the information in Part II and Part III will help), create an assessment list by placing each skill required into one of the following categories:

Knowledge and Skills
You already possess
You need to acquire before you begin your business
You need to *improve* before you begin your business
You can purchase

This assessment is an important step in your business planning. It helps to inventory the knowledge and skills you have and those you need to acquire. For example, a partial assessment list for an Internet store might look something like this:

Knowledge/Skills I need	Source
How to register my business name	Already possess
How to use a computer	Already possess
How to build my website	Purchase (hire)
How to maintain my website	Acquire
How to price inventory	Acquire
How to find customers	Improve
How to manage my time	Improve

Bumps in the Road

The road to business success is paved with bumps. Being well-prepared will help you get over many of them, but sooner or later, you're bound to hit a few. Perhaps a popular supplier refuses to deal with your home-based business and another requires expensive minimum orders. The water heater spews over a good part of your inventory, and your only employee calls in sick just as you're taking Junior to his soccer game. Expect the unexpected. The more you prepare for bumps, the more likely you'll be able to handle them.

Some business days are better than others. It's easy to stay motivated on the good days, when you make a big sale, when a customer is thrilled with the album you created, and when things sail along without a hitch. It's the not-so-good days that can sap your energy and enthusiasm. Find ways to stay motivated. Review your goals and visualize what it will be like when you achieve them. If your goal is to make enough income to take the family to Hawaii, post a picture of an island beach at sunset where you can see it every day. Focus on the positives and find ways of dealing with the negatives. Manage stress before it makes a big dent in your motivation. Arm yourself with knowledge and skills. When a bump appears before you, find a way to go around it.

Win Your Family's Support

How does your family feel about your business idea? Is your spouse supportive? Who will be there when your kids get home from school? Before you begin your endeavor, sit down with your family and discuss your ideas. Describe why you want to begin your business, and how your success will benefit the entire family. Address your spouse's skepticism and your children's worries.

Help your family understand you're serious about succeeding. Solicit their opinions to see how chores can be redistributed on certain days to free time for you. Assure them you won't be a stranger and that your first commitment is to them. You might even involve them in your effort. Maybe your spouse can help with bookkeeping, website maintenance, or other special skills. If your kids are old enough for responsibility, perhaps they'll enjoy the experience of working with you. By sharing your ideas with your family and addressing their concerns, you can turn your business into a positive experience for the entire family.

Part II:
Finding the
Right Business

- ⦿ The Home Store
- ⦿ The Retail Store
- ⦿ The Internet Store
- ⦿ Scrapbook Consultant
- ⦿ Commissioned Scrapbooker
- ⦿ Teacher
- ⦿ Event Planner
- ⦿ Product Designer / Developer
- ⦿ Writer

I think I can, I think I can.—*The Little Engine That Could*

Chapter 4.
The Home Store

Start-up cost:	$500 and up
Income potential:	Low to moderate
Commitment:	Part-time or full-time
Financial risk:	Low to moderate

Sixty percent of all U.S. businesses start at home. And why not? Working from home gives you a flexibility no other job can match: you can chart your own professional course, work in your jammies, and schedule business around Little League games and PTA meetings. You make all the decisions, keep all the profits, and have the best possible commute.

There are some potential downsides to working at home. As a one-person business you play all the roles. Besides being the boss, you're the bookkeeper, accountant, secretary, shipping clerk, and janitor. You may miss the social interaction of working with others, or discover you're a workaholic who can't find time to do the laundry or mow the lawn.

Do Things on the Up and Up

Before you set up shop, make sure it's legal for you to operate a business from your residence. If you rent your home, read your lease or rental agreement to determine whether businesses are allowed. Talk with your city clerk about obtaining a city business license. Most local licenses can be obtained by filling out an application and paying a minimal fee (usually between $10-$100) which is renewed annually.

Remember those road bumps mentioned back in Chapter 3? One of the first you encounter may be a local ordinance restricting or prohibiting home businesses. Long ago many cities established such laws to preserve the serenity of residential areas. Unfortunately, although home businesses are now commonplace, many of these archaic laws remain on the books. If you find your neighborhood isn't zoned for retail businesses, don't give up. Ask if any type of home businesses is allowed and see how yours can fit. If you still run into resistance, point out the following:

■ Your business will be no different than the home-based Avon and Tupperware demonstrators who currently operate in your city.

■ Unlike retail storefronts, you won't post signs or have regular shopping hours when customers come and go, so your business won't create excess traffic or noise. Explain that your supplies will be delivered by UPS or FedEx couriers—a common sight in most neighborhoods.

■ You won't have employees.

■ Your sales will be made through the mail or over the Internet (of course, don't mention this if it doesn't apply).

If all else fails, request a variance. This usually means the city gives your neighbors an opportunity to comment on your proposed business. Explain your plan to your neighbors (potential new customers!), and ask them to sign a petition allowing your business to exist. Think about mounting a campaign to have the outdated laws changed. In the meantime, apply for a license to sell your products at group workshops, seminars, crops, or other events you coordinate.

Find a Space to Call Your Own

If you're serious about starting a home business, you need room to store inventory, do administrative work, and, if appropriate, a place to meet customers. Perhaps you can use the spare bedroom or clear the clutter from the attic or basement. Park outside and use the garage (be sure to keep inventory dry). If no other space is available, convert a closet. Don't laugh! Many people turn closets into their own private space. Install good lighting (recessed lighting will save space), paint the walls white to reflect light, hang some cheery artwork, mount a workspace, and cover the walls with shelves or cabinets.

If you live in small quarters or your house is already cramped for space, be resourceful and go with what you have. Many businesses have been launched from kitchen tables, where "office hours" begin before the household awakes or after the dinner dishes are done. It may not be ideal, but you can make it work.

Ask the family to respect your work area. That means a pet-free zone that is off-limits to toy trucks, TV, and dirty laundry. As much as possible, treat your business space as you would a rented office; keep non-business items elsewhere.

Start Organized, Stay Organized

Whether your workspace is a spare room or the coffee table, you'll be more productive if you're orderly and organized. Good organization—knowing where everything is and the ability to find it quickly—saves time and frustration. It's even more important when you don't have a dedicated business location in the house.

Dealing with Distractions

● While working on your business, resist the temptation to watch Oprah, play with the dog, or engage in other non-business activities.

● Let the answering machine take calls on the family telephone, unless it's also your business line.

● Create a to-do list of business tasks you want to accomplish each day. Stay focused on one task until it's complete, then move on to another.

Adequate inventory storage and display space is critical for a home-based business. You can't sell your collection of foil papers if they're torn or crumpled from being stuffed in a drawer. Imagine digging through boxes desperately trying to find that circle cutter while an impatient customer looks on.

Pizza Anyone?

Julie Creek of Creek Bank Creations buys new unmarked pizza boxes for 45¢ each from her local pizza parlor. The boxes provide perfectly flat storage for customers' paper purchases at her home store. Julie's neighbors want to know why everyone leaves her house with a pizza! Contact: (217) 427-2578 or dreamn_1@yahoo.com.

Inventory on Wheels

Rubbermaid carts with see-through drawers make great portable storage bins. You can simply roll them from room to room as needed. The shallow drawers and compartments of rollaround tool bins make good storage containers too—sometimes you can find them at garage sales.

If closet and shelf space is nonexistent in your house, be creative. Use hanging files or inexpensive transparent storage boxes. Search garage sales for old armoires, storage chests, dressers, or cabinets.

Maintain an orderly filing system for materials. Sort die cuts and stickers by theme in photo boxes, or insert them into page protectors in three-ring binders. Home improvement stores sell tool and bait boxes with adjustable partitions; they're handy for storing punches, scissors, adhesives, and other small scrapbooking accessories. Consider tilt bins and storage tools made for scrappers.

If you're really cramped for space, create a "business box" for your administrative materials. File all your brochures, invoices, sales receipts, customer records, tax information and other administrative paperwork in labeled folders, and store them in a sturdy storage box with a well-constructed lid. Then store the box up on a closet shelf, under the bed, or in any other easily-accessible spot that is out of the way of normal household traffic and curious little ones.

More Issues to Consider

The fact that you're operating a business from your home shouldn't detract from your professionalism. Treat your customers courteously and professionally—they may not know that you're taking their telephone orders in your bathrobe or speaking to them while your kids are feeding the goldfish to the dog. Here are a few other business issues to keep in mind:

Schedule business time. Set regular business hours for yourself. If your schedule is erratic, make a goal to work a consistent number of hours each week—then do it.

Get to know your customers. Who are your customers and how will you find them? What type of products and services will they buy? How do you plan to make your business known? Will you sell products locally, via the Internet, or by mail order?

Six Ways to Make Time for Your Business

1. Give up TV, bowling, or some other activity (not scrapping, of course).

2. Consolidate chores and errands to free up a few hours of business time.

3. Ask family members to share more responsibilities around the house.

4. Consider getting a cleaning lady or a gardener—really!

5. Cancel unnecessary magazine subscriptions.

6. Spend less time on the phone.

Provide additional services. Increase your customer base and sell more inventory by creating albums for others, teaching classes, or launching an Internet store. Coordinate and sponsor crops, swaps, or other cropping events. Publish a newsletter to stay in touch with customers.

Manage Your Inventory

As an avid scrapper, you probably already have a bad case of buying fever. You just can't seem to help yourself. You pick up a few albums, buy several rolls of stickers, and collect papers like they're going out of style (maybe some of them are). Before you know it, you've invested several mortgage payments in an ever-growing, out-of-control inventory that spills out of every drawer and closet in the house.

Check out the competition before you buy and stock your inventory. Will customers buy your heart punch for $4.99 when Michael's sells it for $3.99? Check K-Mart, Target, Wal-Mart, office supply stores, the local scrapbooking, craft, and photo stores, and any other stores selling scrapbooking items in your area.

Take a look at what these stores sell and how they price each item. Don't forget to include Internet scrapbooking stores. They're competitors too.

If you live in an area with little or no competition, you're lucky. Even if you're not the only game in town, you can still find ways to compete against the big guys:

- Build an inventory of albums, speciality papers, tools, stickers, kits or supplies your competitors don't sell.

Getting a Head Start

Kimberly Ottosen of Handcart Heritage Albums built her customer base six months *before* she opened her home-based store. She started by inviting scrappers to free monthly classes during which they could buy products. Satisfied participants told friends, and soon Kimberly had 25 regular customers. By the time she launched her store—cleverly scheduled to coincide with National Scrapbooking Day— Kimberly already had pre-orders from eager customers. Contact: (281) 531-4484 or handcartheritage@yahoo.com.

Or stock some of the items they do, so you can sell those to customers when they buy your specialty items—be a one-stop shopping experience for your customers.

■ Offer knowledge and expertise, something the larger stores rarely do. Let your customers know you're ready, willing, and able to answer their questions about products and techniques, and you're happy to make suggestions regarding their album themes or page layouts.

■ Take your business to your customers. Consider offering free home delivery, or delivery at no charge with a minimum purchase.

■ Coordinate papers, borders, stickers, and other materials by color or theme and sell them as kits or grab bags. Many scrapbookers appreciate time-saving techniques; create seasonal and themed kits of coordinated papers, borders, stickers and other materials.

Another one of those bumps you'll discover is the reluctance of many popular suppliers to do business with you. Some feel home-based and Internet stores undercut the sales of scrapbook storefronts. Others may require minimum purchases that seriously strain your budget. Here are three ways to detour around these buying bumps:

■ Contact the manufacturer or supplier and ask for their wholesale terms. If they aren't keen on selling to a home store, offer to pay in advance and furnish evidence of your spotless credit history.

■ Contact other wholesale distributors to find out who may carry the same product. Ask for their catalogs and wholesale terms.

■ Join in with other small scrapbook retailers to get discounted prices from wholesalers and suppliers. (See *More Home Store Resources* on the following page for information on group buys.)

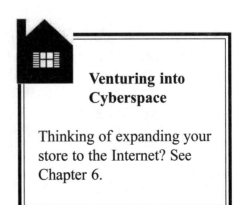

Venturing into Cyberspace

Thinking of expanding your store to the Internet? See Chapter 6.

More Home Store Resources

Books and Publications

- *At Home At Work: The Newsletter for Parents Who Work from Home* (508) 634-3989

- *Home Office Magazine* (800) 274-6229 or www.homeofficemag.com

- *The Home Office and Small Business Answer Book* by Janet Attard

- *Ideas for Great Home Offices* (Sunset Publishing)

- *101 Home Office Secrets* by Lisa Kanarek

- *Working from Home* and *Working from Home: Everything You Need to Know To Live and Work Under the Same Roof* by Paul and Sarah Edwards

- *Working Solo* by Teri Lonier. Also online at www.workingsolo.com

On the Internet

- The Internet has tons of helpful information and ideas for home-based entrepreneurs, including Bizy Moms.com (www.bizymoms.com), Her Home Office (www.herhomeoffice.com), Home-based Working Moms (www.hbwm.com), Moms Network (www.momsnetwork.com), The Parentpreneur Club (www.parentpreneurclub.com), and Work At Home Mom.com (www.wahm.com)

- Log on to www.groups.yahoo.com and subscribe to Scrapping4others and 4scrapbookretailers to participate in group buys with other small scrapbook retailers. New groups are created all the time, so check the site frequently; just search for "retail scrapbook." The Retail Latte message board at www.jangle.com is another good source of group buys and general information from scrapbook entrepreneurs

You can't expect to hit the jackpot if you don't put a few nickels in the machine.—Flip Wilson

 ## Chapter 5.
The Retail Store

Start-up cost:	High
Income potential:	High
Commitment:	Full-time
Financial risk:	High

Owning a retail store is the ultimate dream for many scrappers. Just imagine stocking shelves with endless new products, thanking happy customers for their patronage, and seeing your profits grow month after month. Is this a realistic vision or a fantasy?

Reality: The Good, the Bad, and the Ugly

Succeeding in any retail business is tough, and scrapbooking is no exception. The risks are substantial, but the profits can be as well. Realizing your dream instead of a nightmare of loss and frustration, involves hard work and long hours with liberal doses of stress tossed in for good measure. It also takes commitment, limitless enthusiasm, energy, and cash... lots and lots of cash. New stores open every month. Some aren't in business long, because many scrappers don't realize the complexities of operating a retail store. Their hearts are in the right place, and they may create excellent album pages, but their business preparation is often inadequate.

So, what's the difference between scrappers who spend sleepless nights worrying about failure, and those who run not one, but several stores successfully—and enjoy doing it? The difference certainly includes motivation and a positive attitude. Primarily, though, it's good planning. If planning is important to other scrapbooking businesses, it's absolutely critical for a retail store. With the possible exception of product development, retail stores require bigger start-up investments, and larger risks, and have greater income potential than any other scrapbooking business. How successful do you think the following two entrepreneurs will be? (These are real comments!)

Conversation overheard:

Woman #1: I'm going to start a business in that vacant storefront on Main Street.
Woman #2: How wonderful! What kind of business?
Woman #1: A scrapbooking store.
Woman #2: Oh, how long have you been scrapbooking?
Woman #1: Well, I've never actually done a scrapbook, but I know scrapbooking is very popular right now.

Posting to a scrapbook message board:

I really want to open a scrapbooking store in my town. I'm a very good scrapper. I have no business experience and the store rentals are very expensive. I doubt if I could make a profit, but I want to go ahead.

Huh? No planning, no experience...no sales! In the first example, Woman #1 has no scrapbooking skills or knowledge, doesn't know if she has a market, and probably doesn't have any business skills. The person in the second example recognizes the danger signs but chooses to ignore them. Both of these business ideas are disasters waiting to happen.

Now for the good news. You *can* make your dream happen. Others succeed at this business, and you can too, if you're willing to make the required commitment. Give yourself enough time to adequately prepare. You wouldn't enter a race with one leg tied to the other; don't handicap your business efforts by being unprepared. The best planning in the world can't prepare you for every customer, product, or vendor issue you'll experience. But good preparation will show you what to expect, and how to react when unexpected problems occur...and they will occur.

Survey Says!

- Hours per week scrapbook retailers spend in store:
  60 hours or more: 21%
  41-60 hours: 40%
  20-40 hours: 28%
  1-19 hours: 11%

- Hours per week scrapbook retailers spend on business outside the store:
  1-10 hours: 61%
  11-20 hours: 23%
  21 hours or more: 16%

Do the goals you identified back in Chapter 2 support or conflict with the long hours and financial commitment of running a retail store? Are you willing to trade a 40-hour work week for a 60 to 70-hour work week? Can you afford to work your business for two, three, or more years before you break even and start earning a paycheck? Do you have the patience and professional stamina to grow your business and invest profits back into the store?

Experience is the Best Teacher

Store owner Kim Amond believes you gain valuable experience by first retailing on a small scale. Her years as a consultant and home-store owner taught her to manage inventory, deal with competition, forge customer and vendor relationships, and promote her business. This experience gave her the priceless knowledge and skills she used to start her retail store, Heirlooms from the Heart. Contact (315) 451-2781.

Will you be a happy camper when it's time to stock shelves, train employees, pay suppliers, deal with the landlord, and keep your business records current? Ask yourself these questions before you begin. If you decide a retail store is the right business for you, learn all you can. Do it right, do it well, and believe in your own power to succeed.

You Have to Spend Money to Make Money

Anyone who wants to start a store has two important questions: how much do I need and how much will I make? No single answer applies to everyone

---

Survey Says!

- Start-up cost of retail scrapbook store:
  Less than $10,000: 39%
  $10,000 to $49,000: 29%
  $50,000 to $100,000: 24%
  More than $100,000: 7%

- Method of funding:
  Savings, credit cards, or other personal assets: 40%
  Funding from personal assets and partner: 29%
  Loan from a bank, credit union, or other lender: 19%
  Loan from family: 10%

- Average monthly income from store (before expenses):
  Less than $1,000 per month: 30%
  $1,000 to $3,000: 18%
  $4,000 to $6,000 per month: 22%
  $10,000 or more: 30%

- Average monthly profit (after expenses):
  Doesn't make enough to pay monthly expense: 9%
  Makes only enough to cover monthly expenses: 45%
  Makes a monthly profit: 45%

and all circumstances, but here are some of the key issues that impact start-up costs and profit.

The size of your store. With little exception, small stores make small profits. Underfund in the beginning, or invest in a location with inadequate space, and you limit your profit potential. The overhead and investment is certainly less in a small shop (1,000 square feet or fewer); many consultants recommend at least 2,000 to 2,500 square feet to make a profit worthy of your effort and investment.

Survey Says!

● Size of retail scrapbook stores:
1,000 square feet or fewer: 45%
1,500 to 3,000 square feet: 48%
3,000 to 4,000 square feet: 5%
More than 4,000 square feet: 2%

In addition to inventory space, you'll need adequate room for additional services you plan to offer. If you're depending on classes to provide a portion of your income, you'll need enough space to accommodate students comfortably. If you plan to attract customers with product demonstrations, die-cut machines, a cropping room, or a children's play area, take those requirements into consideration when shopping for store space.

Inventory management. The most critical business decision is what products you'll sell. Hopefully, you'll base that decision on market research and practical experience. Me & my BIG ideas stickers, heart punches, and Journaling Genie will fly off the shelves, while other products may seem to be glued to the shelves.

Survey Says!

● What store owners wish they knew before starting their stores:
More about business skills: 50%
More about time and stress management: 27%
More about balancing business and family committments: 16%
More about scrapbooking: 3%

Inventory profit is made in two ways: sell fewer products with greater profit margin, or more products with smaller margins. In truth, your sales will be a combination of both. You need an inventory of products people want. Some will sell better than others, and some will be more profitable than others. Generally, just 20% of your customers will provide 80% of your business. Let their interests most influence your purchasing decisions.

Check Out the Competition

Scout the competition before you tour vacant store space. Who are they, what do they sell, and how do they price products? How will their business impact yours? Assess the impact of competitors on your ability to succeed:

■ Local merchants. This includes any business selling scrapbooking supplies, including scrapbooking stores; gift boutiques; craft stores; photo shops; drug stores; discount stores like Target, Wal-Mart, and K-Mart; and home-based businesses.

■ QVC and the Home Shopping Network.

■ Direct sale scrapbooking consultants (see Chapter 7 for more information).

■ Internet stores. Your e-competitors don't have the overhead you do, so they can afford to sell the same products at lower prices. They provide customers with plenty of layouts, ideas, and networking with other scrappers. These stores are open 24 hours a day, seven days a week. But their customers can't examine products or get face-to-face help designing album pages— that's your advantage.

■ Mail order catalogs, including Lillian Vernon and Current.

If you're not the first store in your area, how will you add value to the market? If you're lucky enough to be the first, how will you compete when a new Michael's opens at the local mall and advertises 30-40% discounts, or when a scrapbooking store opens just around the corner? To succeed, customers must perceive better value in your service. Stock a broader inventory. Offer lower prices and better service. Sponsor unique crops, classes, and demos. Reward frequent buyers.

Build a base of loyal, satisfied customers who return again and again and who encourage their friends to do the same.

Three Ways to Start a Store

No matter what you're selling, there are three ways to start a retail store:

Start from scratch. With or without a partner, you do all the necessary planning and research for your business, determine which products to sell, set prices, and decide how your profits will be spent. Most start-ups begin this way.

Recipe for Success

Follow Paula Siebers' example if you want a blueprint for retail success. In 1997, after two years of teaching scrapbooking classes and selling products from home, *Woman's Day* profiled Paula's business. In response to the article, people all over the country called her wanting to scrap their own memories. Presented with a rare opportunity, Paula expanded her business to include mail order sales. Soon her growing inventory demanded more space, so Paula moved her business to an in-law apartment next door. This allowed her to set regular business hours and devote an area to classes. Just one year later, in 1998, Paula opened her fully-stocked retail store in Canton, Connecticut. Today, New England Scrapbook Company employs more than 12 employees and instructors, stocks a huge inventory, and offers many daytime and evening classes. Using each business opportunity as a stepping stone to her retail store, Paula gained experience each time her business grew. By the time she opened her store, she was well-versed in inventory issues, business financials, recordkeeping, marketing, customer service, and other skills critical to her retail success. Contact (860) 693-9197 or www.newenglandscrapbook.com.

Buy an existing business.
The opportunity to buy an
existing store might be a
blessing in disguise or a burden
disguised as a blessing. Proceed with the caution of
Sherlock Holmes. Why is the
owner selling? Is she moving
away, or did poor manage-
ment and low profits drive her
to sell?

Get on the List!

Creating Keepsakes and *Memory Makers* provide retail store directories in their magazines and on their websites. See the publications, www.creatingkeepsakes.com and www.memorymakersmagazine.com.

Be mindful of the baggage you
may assume with the business. What are the lease terms and restrictions? Is the
space adequate for your needs? What type of investment is required to get the
store the way you want it? Is the existing inventory what you want to sell? Has it
been selling well? How do fix-up and start-up costs compare with starting a
store from scratch? On what factors has the asking price been based?

Check with the Chamber of Commerce about the store's local image. Ask
suppliers about the store's credit status. How much debt does the store owe?
Review vendor invoices. Hire an accountant to review financial records and tax
returns for the past three to four years. Identify and understand the store's
overall sales, growth pattern, management efficiency, and other critical information. Retain a lawyer to review the purchase agreement.

Store-in-a box: the franchise option. Buying a franchise, like a Burger King
or Jiffy Lube, is a common way of starting a business. In exchange for an initial
investment and a percentage of your ongoing income, a franchise company
typically provides use of its name, a specific product line, corporate advertising,
training and continuing support.

A franchise doesn't guarantee success, but it may provide the extra support you
need to confidently start your business. Be cautious if you come across a scrapbook franchise opportunity if you're researching store possibilities. Make sure
you're dealing with a solid company that will be around when you need them.
Both of the two scrapbook franchises listed in the first edition of this book are
now out of business. Research everything carefully and be sure you understand

all the implications and requirements. Weigh the advantages, disadvantages, and overall cost of franchising compared to other alternatives. Franchise agreements are complex and legally binding; always involve an attorney and an accountant.

Know Your Rights

Franchise companies are licensed by the state in which they do business, and they must provide the Franchisor's Disclosure (also referred to as the Franchise Offering Circular) to potential franchisees. This document discloses franchise costs, terms, and conditions. The franchisor is also required to provide a list of the names, addresses, and telephone numbers of prior franchisees.

Retail Store Consultants

If you're willing to pay a fee, a few seasoned scrapbook store owners will share their retail expertise with you. These companies don't do your planning for you, but they can tell you what running a scrapbook store is really like. They can also point you in the right direction with "insider information" about selecting a location, choosing the right product mix, creating a business plan, learning about retail finances, and many other issues specific to starting and operating a successful store. If you're not sure where to start, or whether a retail store is the right business choice for you, consider attending one of these seminars.

This firsthand information will either convince you to go ahead with your idea or to abandon it altogether. Either way, it's money well spent if you are looking for a starting place. You'll still have a lot of planning and preparation ahead of you, but at least you'll be pointed in the right direction.

Many scrapbook store owners have started retail consulting businesses as an extension of their own successful endeavors. Many start, but not many stick to consulting. The following three consultants have consistently offered retail consulting for several years. Contact each of them for a current description of fees, services, and references.

The Memory Group, LLC. These consultants provide retail training geared specifically for scrapbook stores. TMG's three-day seminars provide comprehensive details about scrapbook retailing. Seminar participants who open their own stores may purchase a "new store inventory kit" of discounted products (delivered to stores with a step-by-step placement guide and point-of-sale inventory database), and take advantage of negotiated discounts with many well-known wholesale suppliers. Contact (734) 759-8642 or log on to www.thememorygroupllc.com.

Crafters Home. Experienced entrepreneurs Norm and Dianna Carlson have helped more than 115 independently-owned stores in the U.S., Puerto Rico, Canada, Australia and the United Kingdom open under the Crafters Home Trademark Licensing Agreement.

The Crafters Home consulting fee includes two days of training at the corporate offices in Scottsdale, Arizona, help with your business plan, access to forms, policies and procedures, and direct purchasing agreements from manufacturers and distributors. Contact (800) 486-3534 or www.craftershome.biz.

The Scrapbook Connection. This consulting group offers information, support, training, and negotiated vendor discounts to owners of any type of scrapbooking business, including retail stores. The company's goal is to help any scrapreneur succeed, whatever her business. Members may participate in group buys and take advantage of lower dollar minimums by using the Product Vendor Alliance. The organization's website provides opportunities to share ideas and encouragement with e-mail lists, member chat rooms, auctions, and other online events. The Mentor Program matches fledgling store owners with more experienced members. Contact (888)573-0556 or visit the website at www.thescrapbookconnection.com.

Location, Location, Location

The old adage about buying a home also applies to your business location. The three most important elements are location, followed by location, and then location. The spot you choose for your retail business can make or break your business, so select it wisely. If customers can't find you, or don't like the neighborhood when they do find you, they probably won't be back. Determine whether the property is large enough to provide the services and inventory you need to meet your profit projections.

Observe foot traffic in front of the space on different days of the week and at different hours of the day to judge potential walk-in business. Are the plumbing, cooling, heating, and other features adequate and in working order? Will you need to repaint, recarpet, or entirely remodel? Who pays for your changes? What are the zoning laws? Under what lease conditions may you or the landlord make changes or terminate? Schedule a visit from the building inspector to ensure the space is up to code. Draft layouts to determine the best use of your floor space. Is the store affordable, yet large enough to carry an appealing and competitive inventory?

Check the outside as carefully as the inside. Is parking adequate? Does the store front need repainting, repairs, or new windows? Can you prominently display your store signage?

Get Paid for Practice

If you're unsure about taking the plunge into retail ownership, or you'd like to see what retail scrapbooking is really like before you invest, try working for someone else. Working in a scrapbook store can provide invaluable insight, experience, new friends...and discounted supplies. Your first-hand experience should be enough to convince you to proceed full steam ahead or reconsider your plans to open a store.

Stock the Shelves

The right inventory includes products customers want at prices they're willing to pay. A profitable inventory has a healthy margin (the difference between the wholesale and retail prices), and quick turnover (it sells soon after it goes on display). Here are a few important things to know about inventory:

Considering Mall Space?

Check your store lease agreement before signing. It may dictate the hours your store must be open for business.

Learn the ropes. Managing inventory can be a confusing, complex, and time-consuming effort. Benefit by learning the nuances and tricks of the retail trade early in your planning. Become familiar with margins, markups, turnovers, and distribution channels before starting your store.

Buy from wholesale suppliers. Develop a list of the products you want to stock, then contact vendors to ask for their wholesale price list, credit terms, and minimum requirements. If possible, buy direct from the manufacturer to get the best wholesale prices. Ask if they provide any support materials, and whether you'll be notified of new products. If you buy from distributors, compare prices, shipping costs, and delivery times.

Start off on the right professional foot. Maintain good relationships and pay your bills on time. Attend trade shows and expos, where you can often find special discounts and meet suppliers in person. If a particular manufacturer requires minimum purchases that are too rich for your budget, take advantage of the alternative purchasing ideas discussed in Chapter 4.

Order the right product mix. You have to know what your customers want before you order and stock your inventory. Popular items in Rhode Island may not move well in California. Rural customers may have different preferences than city dwellers. Older customers often look for different patterns and colors than younger scrappers. Will you limit your inventory to basic products for beginning scrappers, or include crimpers, elegant vellums, and mulberry papers? Which tools, die-cuts, scissors, punches, and stickers will you carry?

Survey Says!

● Time spent by retailers working on their own scrapbooks since starting their stores:
No time: 16%
Less time: 61%
Same as before: 18%
More time: 5%

Order products to promote holidays, special occasions, and local events.

Stock up on pastel papers for new moms and cardstock in local team colors. Find innovative ways to market your inventory to your customers' needs and interests. Price your inventory to provide a reasonable profit while being attractive to customers.

Point-of-Sale Software. You'll save time and headaches by investing in a point-of-sale (POS) system: an automated method of managing your inventory. A POS system automatically tracks your product supply by integrating the inventory database and the cash register. First you establish a database of your start-up inventory in the POS, then enter all subsequent transactions. The system increases your inventory records when you enter a store purchase, and decreases it when you enter a store sale. It will also notify you when it's time to reorder products. If you're careful about keeping your POS up-to-date, it can greatly minimize the time you spend on accounting, recordkeeping, and tax preparation.

At any given time, you can quickly determine which products are selling and which aren't, identify customer buying patterns (handy for frequent buyer reward programs), and view many other useful indicators.

POS-in-a-Box

O'Brien Solutions offers a POS designed for scrapbooking stores. It comes with a database of more than 50,000 product codes for 300 vendors. Contact (714) 342-1904 or www.obriensolutions.com.

What About Employees?

If you're going to open a store, you'll need help serving customers, stocking shelves, teaching classes, making display pages, and maintaining all the other activities that keep your business alive. The number of employees you'll need depends on your store size, services provides, and your operating hours.

There's a big difference between employees who want to be part of your team and employees who simply show up for paychecks. Customers will become frustrated if your employees aren't familiar with the products they sell. You want scrappers as employees—people who love scrapbooking and enthusiastically answer customers' questions about tools, techniques, and products.

Scrappers are often eager to work part-time in exchange for moderate wages and a discount on materials. But don't expect even the most enthusiastic workers to know what you want. Be clear about your expectations. Do you want them to greet customers immediately, or let them browse? Show employees how to use the point-of-sale software, and clearly explain other tasks for which they're responsible. Establish a team atmosphere, where it's fun to come to work. Prepare employees to accept more responsibilities so you can attend to other important issues. Provide regular recognition for a job well done and take corrective action when appropriate and necessary.

Survey Says!

- How owners staff their stores:
  Owner only: 29%
  Unpaid family/friends: 16%
  Paid employees: 31%
  Paid family/friends: 24%

- Number of *paid* employees:
  One employee: 30%
  Two employees: 15%
  Three employees: 26%
  Four - six employees: 29%

- Number of *unpaid* employees:
  One employee: 31%
  Two employees: 46%
  Three employees: 8%
  Four or five employees: 0%
  Five or more employees: 15%

More Retail Store Resources

The Small Business Administration (SBA). One of the best (and free) resources available is the Small Business Administration. The SBA's sole purpose is to nurture and counsel American small business. The agency provides counselors, videos, books, software, online tutorials, and classroom seminars. Visit your local SBA office of contact (800) 827-5722 or www.sba.gov. The SBA also sponsors several related business services:

- **Business Information Centers (BICs).** Anyone interested in starting a business can use the reference library, videos, computers, and other equipment at these one-stop business centers. Experienced onsite counselors also provide advice. Contact your local SBA office or visit www.sba.gov/bi/bics

- **Small Business Development Centers (SBDCs).** More than 1,000 U.S. SBDCs provide hands-on business and technical assistance. Contact (202) 205-6766 or www.sba.gov/regions/states.html to find the SBDC nearest you

- **The Service Corps of Retired Executives (SCORE).** More than 12,000 retired business managers provide advice, counsel, and mentoring to prospective and active small business owners. This voluntary group sponsors inexpensive workshops on a variety of critical business issues and skills. Counseling and information are available by telephone, e-mail, or in person. Call (800) 634-0245 or log on to www.score.org to locate a chapter near you or submit a request for counseling

Small business incubators. More than 80% of incubator graduates go on to start successful businesses. Incubators offer workshops, counseling, and other services to help "hatch" new businesses. Contact your Chamber of Commerce or the National Business Incubation Association at (614) 593-433 or visit www.allbusiness.com

Colleges and universities. Most colleges and universities offer practical education for starting businesses. Check the registration catalog, admissions office, or website

Books and Publications

■ *The Complete Guide to Buying a Business* by Richard Snowden

■ *The E-Myth Revisited* by Michael Gerber

■ *1,001 Ways to Create Retail Excitement* by Edgar A. Falk

■ *Retail In Detail: How To Start and Manage A Small Retail Business* by Ronald L. Bond

■ *So You Want to Open a Retail Store* by Irvin Bursteiner

■ *Specialty Shop Retailing: How To Run Your Own Store* by Carol L. Schroeder

■ *Turning Your Great Idea Into A Great Success* by Judy Ryder

■ *Scrapbook Premier* is a catalog of scrapbook products, sent to all retail scrapbook stores in the U.S., free of charge. Contact (435) 586-1449 or see www.scrapbookpremier.com to sign up for your free copy

On the Internet

■ You'll find plenty of small business information online, including: All Business (www.allbusiness.com), American Express Small Business Exchange (home3.americanexpress.com/smallbusiness), Business Know How (www.businessknowhow.com), and CCH Business Owner's Toolkit (www.toolkit.cch.com)

■ *News Flash!,* an online newsletter from *Creating Keepsakes,* provides tips, ideas, information, and product announcements. Subscribe at www.creatingkeepsakes.com

■ Check out the group buys and message boards mentioned in the previous chapter

The Internet is like a giant jellyfish. You can't step on it. You can't go around it. You've got to get through it.—John Evans

Chapter 6.
The Internet Store

Start-up cost:	Low to moderate
Income potential:	Low to moderate
Commitment:	Moderate
Financial risk:	Low to moderate

With all due respect to baseball, Internet shopping is quickly becoming America's favorite pastime. The e-commerce phenomenon has fundamentally changed the way we shop, and it's here to stay. Selling online is an affordable alternative to a retail storefront, and it's portable—if you relocate, you still keep your business and your customer base. Just consider these statistics:

■ 71% of online buyers are satisfied with the experience and security of shopping online.[1]

■ 54% of all Internet purchases are made in the U.S.[1]

- U.S. e-commerce is expected to top $100 billion by 2003.[2]

- Women make almost half of all Internet purchases in the U.S.[3]

[1] Source: Angus Reid Group (1999), [2] eMarketer (2000), [3] Bizrate.com

Your customers can shop your website from home or the office, from down the street or around the world. They don't have to travel to you, they don't have to wait in line ...they don't even have to get dressed. Your cybershop is open 24 hours a day, seven days a week, without paying a penny in employee overtime. The Internet levels the retail playing field. You may be operating from your laundry room, but your website can give you an online presence to rival the biggest scrapbook store in the land.

Creating Keepsakes' Online Survey

A recent survey asked why two million people visit *Creating Keepsakes'* website each month:

☑ Looking for product information: 81%

☑ Using the online retail store directory: 70%

☑ Looking for other scrapbook sites: 50%

☑ Buying scrapbooking products: 62%

Is There Room for You on the 'Net?

Scrappers have discovered cybershopping. New Internet scrapbook sites appear with increasing frequency. A few clicks of your mouse and you've entered a gigantic shopping mall of nothing but scrapbook stores. Buying proudcts online is convenient, cost-effective and reliable.

Many of these stores will succeed, while others will fail. Why? Because, although you may be operating your Internet store from home, if you want it to be profitable, you must give it the same attention you would a traditional store on the street or in a mall. That means marketing, pricing, inventory and all the other usual retail responsibilities.

Millions of Potential New Customers

Have a home store or a retail storefront? Expanding your retail operation to the Internet is a cost-effective way to attract more customers and sell more products.

Anyone can create a website. More importantly, you want to create a *profitable* website. You have to first find customers, then give them what they want: good inventory selection, competitive prices, and great service. Like a retail store, your website must be an inviting, well-organized place to shop. Take a look at several online scrapbook stores. (Unlike traditional stores, you can check out your Internet competitors without wearing a disguise!) Some sites, like dMarie (www.dmarie.com) and Cut 'N' Fun (www.cutnfun.com) are well-designed and well-promoted, while others are a hobbyist's afterthought. Which will your site be?

What About Impulse Sales?

Brick-and-mortar store owners aren't the only retailers to enjoy impulse sales. Twenty-five percent of Internet shoppers make impulse sales.

Is there room for your business on the 'Net? The answer is yes. Follow these six steps to get your cyber store going.

Step 1. Get connected. If you're not already connected to the Internet, get a computer with a modem and shop around for an Internet Service Provider (ISP) with competitive monthly rates and good technical support.

Step 2. Surf and plan. Visit several retail and scrapbooking sites with both a customer's and a competitor's perspective. Notice how information is displayed. As you surf and study, list the weaknesses and strengths you see. What products do the sites display and what prices do they list? Do they offer frequent buyer discounts or other incentives that may impact your ability to profit?

What informational features do they provide? What menu structure seems most logical? Can you quickly find what you want?

Order products from several sites to compare customer service techniques. Armed with your research data, list the products you want to sell and the website features you want to include (see *Features for Retail Websites* later in this chapter). Decide how you'll add value to the market. Develop a business plan for your store (see Chapter 16).

The Name Game

10,000 domains are registered online every day in the U.S.

Step 3. Register your domain. Your domain name—also known as your Universal Resource Locator (URL)—is your Internet address. More than one online company may use the same name, but no two websites may share the same URL. Ideally, your URL should reflect the name of your business, such as "www.scrapbookgarden.com."

Once you choose your URL, visit an Internet registry site (see "Shop Around" at the bottom of this page) to see if your URL of choice is available. If someone else has already registered that name, choose another, or, if there's no web page associated with the URL, contact the registered domain owner to see if he will relinquish his right to the URL. An alternative is to structure the URL with a slight difference. For example, if you find someone else has already registered "www.scrapbookgarden.com," you may decide to register and use

Shop Around

To find an Internet registry site, use your favorite search engine to look for keyword "domain registry." Use any registry site to check the availability of your proposed URL, but compare registration fees. One of the least expensive is www.000domains.com, where you can register your URL for less than $20 a year.

"www.*the*scrapbookgarden.com." The problem with choosing a name that is just a few characters different than another is that you may inadvertently send customers to your competitors. It's better to come up with a descriptive, unique business name with an URL to match.

Step 4. Find a host. A web host is the place where your online store resides. You'll find so many web hosting services, your head will spin! Take the time to research them carefully. Compare prices and services. Know what you're getting—and not getting—for your monthly fee. Determine what extra features are available and supported. Look for web hosts who provide these basic, critical services:

■ Your own domain name.

■ Enough online space to support future growth.

■ Fast-loading pages and graphics.

■ Reliable service with no downtime.

■ Accessible and reliable technical support.

Free Isn't Always Smart

Think twice before you start your store with a free website. Most of these freebies offer little in the way of technical support, retail features, web space, and design, and are unsuitable for retail sites. Unless you pay extra to have your own domain registered, your site's name is usually tacked onto the end of the ISP's own URL, such as: "www.freewebsites.com/scrapbookgarden/html." This type of URL is less likely to be found by surfers, less likely to be typed correctly, and may be ignored by many Internet search engines. In addition, many shoppers associate this type of store URL with amateur retailers.

Step 5. Design and build your site. When you know which products you want to sell, and how you'll price them, you're ready to build and stock your cyber store. It doesn't have to be expensive, but your store should be well-organized, inviting, and easy for visitors to point, click, and buy. There are three ways to create your online webstore:

■ **Do it yourself.** Knowing how to create your own website is a tremendous advantage. You'll save the expense of paying someone else to do it, and you'll be able to make your own frequent changes as you add new products and information (some website designers make take a day or two to make a simple five-minute change and charge you for it). Become a 'Net nerd. Learn to use Hyper Text Markup Language (HTML)—the web development language. It's not as difficult as you may think. Attend a class, take an online tutorial or visit the library. You can also use English language interfaces like Adobe Pagemill or Microsoft Frontpage, but they're not as functionally robust as HTML and often can't be viewed by all Internet browsers.

■ **Hire a professional.** Consider hiring a pro to design your site; look online or in the telephone directory under 'Internet' or "Web Design." Or contact the webmaster of any sites you particularly like (an e-mail or link to the developer is usually posted at the bottom of the web page). A less expensive but often satisfactory option is to hire a technology student from your local college or university. Be sure to discuss his qualifications, be very clear about what you want, and agree in writing to the payment terms and due date.

What Could Be Better...

...than having a scrapper and expert web designer all rolled into one? John Hanson of Webmasters will create your custom website, whether it's a single-page or complete online ordering system. He'll also help you find the right web host, register your domain name, and submit your site to search engines for optimum exposure. See an example of John's work at www.cutnfun.com, a site run by his wife Carrie. Contact (888) 828-8638 or webmasters@cutnfun.com.

■ **Hire someone to build it; you make future changes.** You can have an expert create your site, then learn to make changes yourself. Maybe you have a friend or brother-in-law who's a whiz at web design and will be happy to create your website in exchange for babysitting, a couple of pies, or even a custom scrapbook.

■ **Use an e-commerce provider.** Even 'Net novices can have their stores operating in a jiffy. Plenty of web hosts provide what-you-see-is-what-you-get tools and templates (so you don't have to know HTML) to quickly customize your own store. Some offer free websites in exchange for advertising on your site, or require you to use their credit card merchant to process customer payments. Many offer standard retail site features, then charge for additional services. Most allow you to use your own domain name. Be sure to get a site with enough room for your product photos, text and other information, with plenty of room for your increasing inventory. Compare the cost and features of different web providers by checking the various listings on www.comparewebhosts.com. Carefully read the terms and conditions for each provider before you buy, and always read the fine print.

Step 6. Promote your web store. Who needs Madison Avenue? If you build it well, and promote it well, they will come! The best little webstore in the whole world won't sell an item if no one knows it exists.

Two Good Examples

Looking for examples of well-designed retail scrapbooking sites? Check out Two Peas in a Bucket—don'tcha just love that name?— (www.twopeasinabucket.com) and Keeping Memories Alive (www.keepingmemoriesalive.com). Both sites are well-organized, provide a varied inventory of competitively-priced products, layout ideas, and other information for scrappers. Prices and shipping are clearly stated and customers can easily find what they're looking for.

You have to work just as hard to promote your online store as you would a storefront—maybe more. Submit your URL and key words to Hot Bot, Ask Jeeves, Yahoo, and other major search engines. Or log on to Submit Express (www.submitexpress.com) where you can have your information submitted to 40 major search engines at no charge. Join e-mail lists, newsgroups, and chats to become known in online scrapping circles. Create a signature file to automatically add your URL to your e-mail signature (check your browser manual or e-mail technical support staff). Include your URL on your business cards and other promotional materials. List your store with Jangle (www.jangle.com), Scraplink (www.scraplink.com), and other websites that list Internet scrapbook stores. Spend at least one day a week marketing online to find new customers.

Features for Retail Websites

Here are a few of the most important features that will make life easier for both you and your online shoppers.

.

Shopping cart software. This software makes it easy for customers to add items to a virtual shopping cart as they visit different parts of your website. Each selected item is automatically tallied, so the customer sees a listing of all the items she wants to order, along with the total cost and shipping when she's ready to "check out."

A Safe Alternative

Don't lose customers who are squeamish about posting their credit card information on the 'Net. Suggest they sign-up for Paypal. They post their credit card number with this free service, which electronically "credits" online vendors. Contact www.paypal.com.

Credit card payments. Seventy-five percent of U.S. online shoppers pay with credit cards. If you don't accept credit card payments, you'll lose sales. You can process payments online with software from merchant account providers like ClickBank (www.clickbank.com) or similar vendors who charge an installation fee and a small processing fee for each transaction—an arrangement similar to the merchant accounts retail storeowners traditionally have with banks (see Chapter 15 for more about merchant accounts).

Install software to retain individual customer information, so repeat customers don't have to enter their credit card information every time they order from you.

Website Walk-ins

Is it important to provide information on your retail website? 52% of Internet surfers find websites by looking for information, rather than products.

E-mail. When customers shop at a retail store, they can ask employees about products and techniques, or express their dissatisfaction. Providing "contact us" e-mail extends the same service to your online customers. An automatic e-mail response is handy for thanking customers for placing orders, notifying them of shipping dates, and alerting them to backorder status.

Newsletters. Turn your database of customer e-mail addresses into a powerful marketing tool. Build customer relationships with informational e-newsletters that are well-written, inviting, and not too long. You can certainly use it to announce new products and sales, but the focus should be on information: contests, new ideas for page layouts, new trends. Give customers the option to subscribe to your newsletter; don't just start sending issues to them. Visit www.ezineuniversity.com for tips on writing and using e-newsletters. Manage and automate your newsletter subscription process at www.groups.yahoo.com or search online for "newsletter software."

Surveys. Surveys are fun and allow customers to voice their opinions. Posting a question of the week or the month gives your customers reason to revisit your site. Keep surveys brief and choose broadly appealing topics. Ask visitors what topics they would like addressed, how they make their favorite quick page borders, or how they solve their scrapbooking storage problem. Be sure to post survey results. Write your own survey program, get free survey software from Opinion Power (www.opinionpower.com), or buy Survey Gold (www.surveygold.com).

Contests. Sponsor a monthly or quarterly contest to keep customers coming back to your website. Ask for the best baby page topper, the funniest scrapbooking experience, or the most creative travel layout. Contests should be fun, timely and interesting. Use them to promote holidays and seasonal events.

Ask scrapbook companies to donate products (it's a tax deduction and companies are often glad to get the exposure), and always announce contest winners on your website.

Message boards. Visitors to these online forums log on at their leisure to post questions and share ideas. A busy message board can motivate people to frequently visit your site. Visit www.message-boards.net or search for "create message boards" for more information.

Chats. An online chat is an interactive conversation between scrappers who are simultaneously logged on to your site. Some sites attract participants by scheduling a particular topic or guest during a chat.

Auctions and swaps. Online auctions and swaps are popular ways to buy, sell, and exchange products. Sponsoring sites include Two Peas in a Bucket's For Sale or Trade (www.twopeasinabucket), e-bay (www.ebay.com), and Scrapswap and Trading Everything (find both at groups.yahoo.com).

Tips for Sites that Sell

Content is king. Give scrappers a reason to return frequently to your site to see what's new. Change information frequently. Include tips, layouts, and ideas. Keep product descriptions brief.

Use graphics judiciously. Graphics break up text, add interest, and show what products look like. Use visuals wisely. The larger or more complex the file, the longer customers have to wait to view your webpage.

Don't hide the prices. When you shop you want to know how much things cost, and so will your customers. Establish an easily-understood, easy-to-use order form that clearly states all cost components, including shipping, handling, taxes, and total.

Update your site frequently. Post new ideas and information to encourage repeat visits. Let customers know your site is a place they can count on to stock the newest stickers, die-cuts, paper-piecing kits, or other scrapbooking supplies. Don't make customers search your entire website for something new. Prominently display links to new products and features.

Behind The Scenes

Your online store may require less maintenance and overhead than a store-front, but pay just as much attention to behind-the-scenes operations:

Inventory. The inventory information in Chapters 4 and 5 applies to your online store as well. Stock items that will turnover quickly and provide a healthy profit margin. Frequently compare your product line and prices with those of your competitors.

Customer service. Great service builds customer loyalty. Quality service is just as critical with an online store, if not more so, than being face-to-face with your customers. Even the best inventory and the lowest prices can't make up for a frustrating shopping experience. Take extra steps to satisfy your customers. Always give the option of contacting you by e-mail or telephone. Stand behind your product. Clearly state your policy on refunds and returns. Offer a 100% money-back guarantee if customers aren't satisfied. Respond quickly and professionally to customer concerns, complaints, and questions.

Have policies in place to handle backorders, partial back orders, and customer returns. Let customers know immediately when an item is backordered and when it will be available, or they might look for it somewhere else.

A Taxing Problem

Local and state governments feel they are missing out on valuable revenue as more people shop online. Storefront merchants feel Internet retailers have an unfair advantage by not being required to collect sales tax. Whether Congress will impose taxes on future Internet sales remains to be seen.

If you open a new shipment to find damaged or incorrect products, notify the manufacturer or distributor immediately. Be sure to package shipments adequately so customers will receive undamaged products. Consider additional insurance to cover any potential inventory damage or loss. What will you do when a customer says she never received a product you shipped?

Be prepared for the unexpected. Have a backup plan ready for as many weird happenings as you can imagine. If your computer goes down, your business closes until you're back on line. Keep track of your inventory (use one of the point-of-sale packages mentioned earlier), so you know when to reorder items.

More Ways to Make Money from Your Website

As long as you're going to have a website, why not add to your income? Aside from selling products, there are several ways your website can work for you.

Become an affiliate for another retailer. Experts estimate the Internet will generate $53 billion dollars in revenue by 2003, with 20% going to affiliate programs. Did you know Amazon.com will pay you 15% commission for every customer who buys one of their books through your website? You first enroll, then add the cover graphics and description from any book about scrapping (or others) from Amazon's website. When a visitor to your site clicks on the book, they zoom directly to Amazon's order page. It's a good way to earn income on books without stocking the inventory. Barnesandnoble.com and other companies have similar programs. You can see how this works by visiting www.scraplink.com. Click on "books," then click on any title listed.

Start an affiliate program. Increase sales with your own online sales force. Suggest that other retail and informational sites become your affiliates as described above. Decide first how much you'll pay for each item, and how you'll track the source of referrals to your site. Contact AffiliateZone.com at (877) 689-4255 or www.affiliatezone.com for software that automates the entire process. Once it's installed on your site, it registers potential affiliates, places their information into your databases, and gives them appropriate tracking information. Every subsequent referral and sale is automatically tracked by its source. You just fulfill orders and send the affiliates a monthly check. You get more sales and your affiliates get a no-cost method of additional income. Treat your affiliates fairly and consistently; provide the same promotional materials, information and commission to all of them. You'll improve your bottom line by helping them succeed.

Sell banner ads. Depending who you ask and what you read, banners—those blinking advertisements on the top of websites—are either effective or have overstayed their welcome. Some studies show surfers and shoppers now simply ignore them. Yet banner ads continue to be big business. If you decide to use banners, keep their content related to your site. You can charge someone else to place a banner on your site, but why encourage customers to leave your site as soon as they get there?.

More Internet Store Resources

Books and Publications
- *The Complete Idiot's Guide to Creating a Web Page* by Paul McFedries

- *The Complete Idiot's Guide to E-Commerce* by Robert S. Smith, et. al.

- *The Complete Idiot's Guide to Online Marketing* by William Eager

- *Growing Your Business Online: Small Business Strategies for Working the World Wide Web* by Phaedra Hise

- *Poor Richard's Internet Marketing and Promotions: How to Promote Yourself, Your Business, Your Ideas Online* and *Poor Richards's Website: Geek-Free, Commonsense Advice on Building a Low-Cost Website* by Peter Kent

- *Web Design in a Nutshell* by Jennifer Niederst

On the Internet
- You'll find endless sources of information about websites and the Internet— on the Internet. Learn about website design, marketing, HTML, Internet terminology, and many other cyber issues. Many websites have helpful tutorials and information, including Idea Cafe (www.ideacafe.com), Net Lingo (www.NetLingo.com), Promotion World (www.promotionworld.com), and Web Alley (www.weballey.net)

Small business success comes from 99% perspiration, not the one percent inspiration.—Joe Mancuso

Chapter 7.
Scrapbook Consultant

Start-up investment:	Low to moderate
Income potential:	Low to moderate
Commitment:	Part-time or full-time
Financial risk:	Low to moderate

Consulting is one of the easiest and low-risk scrapbook businesses. Perhaps that's why it's also the most common. There are a few hundred scrapbook stores, but literally thousands of consultants. Because you make money while earning your business training wheels, it's a popular entry-level business.

Being a consultant is like having a mini-retail business without the huge investment of a storefront. You set your own hours, make your own decisions, and work at your own pace. It can be a very good way to make part-time or full-time income doing what you love. Your income depends on the time and effort you devote to your business.

What Does a Consultant Do?

As a consultant, you're a special ambassador for the scrapbooking industry. You get paid for introducing others to the joys of scrapping. You inspire them to preserve their memories and show them how to do it.

Many consultants demonstrate and sell products at home parties or other scrapbooking events. Others create scrapbooks for customers. You may choose to be affiliated with an established direct sales company, selling their products exclusively, and abiding by their rules. Perhaps you prefer working for a scrapbook product company, showing retail stores owners and customers how to use new products. Or you can become an independent consultant, selling any products in any way you wish.

Survey Says!

◉ What consultants do:
teach classes: 39%
sell retail products: 37%
create albums for others: 13%
sell wholesale products: 2%
other: 8%

The choice you make depends on your feelings about the products you sell, and whether you're willing to exchange a part of your income for structure and support. If you're curious about consulting possibilities, first become familiar with each company's products. Decide which best matches your business goals, then contact the organization to request membership information.

Read the terms and conditions carefully before signing up; some organizations have strict rules concerning how their products may be sold. Some organizations require minimum orders or monthly quotas. Weigh the advantages and disadvantages of being an independent compared to being an affiliated consultant:

Survey Says!

◉ Experience as a consultant:
Less than 1 year: 33%
1 to 2 years: 42%
3 to 4 years: 22%
5 years or more: 3%

◉ Consultants planning to
continue their business: 94%

Independent	**Affiliated**
You're a sole proprietor	You're an independent contractor
You buy products at wholesale prices	You buy company products at discounted prices
You develop your own promotional materials	The company may provide some promotional materials
You keep 100% of your profit	A sponsoring consultant may be entitled to a portion of your profit

Whether you're an independent consultant or affiliated with an organization, you're responsible for finding customers, marketing your product, and making sales.

Survey Says!

● Average time per week spent on consulting business:
Less than 5 hours per week: 19%
5 to 10 hours a week: 41%
11 to 30 hours per week: 40%

● Average start-up investment:
Less than $300: 56%
$300 to $499: 18%
$500 to $1,000: 12%
More than $1,000: 13%

● Average monthly consulting income:
Less than $100: 32%
$100 to $299: 40%
$300 to $500: 19%
More than $500: 9%

Close to My Heart (formerly D.O.T.S.)

Close to My Heart sells a full line of exclusive rubber stamping and scrapbooking products through a network of thousands of sales consultants. They earn product discounts and commissions on sales made at home demonstrations. The company rewards consultants for individual sales achievement and, in some circumstances, sales generated by sponsored new recuits.

Founder Jeannette Lynton shares her vision of the company, introduces new products, and offers instructional seminars on various creative techniques at regional events. Consultants receive business and artistic training at the cïmpany's annual convention. Contact (888) 655-6552 or www.closetomyheart.com.

Creative Memories

Founded in 1987 by businesswoman Cheryl Lightle and homemaker Rhonda Anderson, Creative Memories (CM) was the first company to offer archival scrapbooking products directly to consumers through a network of consultants. With almost 50,000 consultants worldwide, CM is now the largest such scrapbooking sales organization. For many people, a CM home demonstration is their introduction to scrapbooking. They fall in love with CM's exclusive product line and become consultants just for the product discount.

Creative Memories is a multi-level direct sales company. As a CM consultant, you purchase products from the company at a discount, then sell them at home parties, much like Avon or Tupperware representatives demonstrate and sell their products. Your entry into the company is sponsored by an existing consultant, who acts as your business mentor and receives a portion of your profits. You, in turn, support any new consultants whom you recruit, and receive a portion of their sales in addition to your own.

Survey Says!

- Consultants whose customers are primarily family, friends, and co-workers: 65%

Contact Creative Memories at (800) 468-9335 or www.creativememories.com.

Creative Marketing

Creative Memories consultant Damian Tredinnick is always looking for ways to expand her business. That's how she came up with the idea for the Real Estate Gift Album Marketing Kit to benefit realtors, homebuyers, and her own business. The kit, which includes a "Welcome Home" page (with a photo of the new house) and a "Thank You" page (with the agent's photo and business card) is presented to homebuyers by agents upon completion of a sale. Damian shows agents how to quickly put pages together for clients, and provides a complimentary workshop voucher for the homeowner to learn how to continue the album. The agent has an appreciative client (and a business write-off), the client has a beautiful memento of the homebuying experience, and Damian gains both the agent and the client as prospective customers. Now *that's* creative marketing.

Life and Times

Established in 1996, Life and Times offers archival scrapbooking products through a network of photojournalist consultants. Consultants purchase albums, pages, page protectors and photo negative storage at a 30% discount, then sell them to others at home parties. The company provides commissions, bonuses and sales incentives. Self-training materials, an online support base and monthly mailings are also available. Contact (800) 852-8873 or www.lifeandtimes.com.

Scrap in a Snap

Scrap in a Snap consultants earn money in two ways: they may purchase the company's scrapbooking products at a discount, then sell them at home parties, or simply pass out catalogs and make a commission on any resulting sales (much like Avon representatives). The company's focus is on sharing products, rather than recruiting new consultants. Contact (866) 462-7627 or www.scrapinasnap.com.

Stampin' Up

Stampin' Up! is a rubber stamp direct sales company, with a program similar to Close to My Heart. Demonstrators buy company products at a 30% discount and sell them directly to customers at home parties. Demonstrators earn commissions and promotions based on their sales and the sales made by recruitees. Accumulated points can be redeemed for gifts and cash awards. Call (800) 782-6787 or visit www.stampinup.com.

The Scrapbook Connection

The Scrapbook Connection offers information and business suport, rather than products. The company's purpose is to help any scrapreneur succeed, whatever her business. For an annual fee, participants receive a training manual to help start and expand their business, teaching software with class handouts and outlines, and two monthly newsletters: one of business ideas and another you can customize and send to your customers. Members may participate in group buys and take advantage of lower dollar minimums by using the Product

---

 Survey Says!

● Consultants affiliated with a direct sales organization: 81%
Creative Memories: 64%
Stampin' Up!: 27%
The Scrapbook Connection: 5%
D.O.T.S.: 4%

● Consultants satisfied with their direct sales organizations:
Very satisfied: 67%
Somewhat satisfied: 27%
Very or somewhat dissatisfied: 6%

Vendor Alliance. The Scrapbook Connection's website provides opportunities to share ideas and encouragement with e-mail lists, member chat rooms, auctions, and other online events. The Mentor Program matches business newbies with experienced members, while the Buddy Program links consultants of similar experience to provide mutual support. Contact (888) 573-0556 or www.thescrapbookconnection.com.

Independent Consultant

You don't have to be affiliated with a sales organization to be a consultant. As an independent consultant, you decide what you sell, where you sell it, and how to price your products and services. You're not bound by company rules or minimum purchase requirements (other than those imposed by wholesale suppliers). Nor are you restricted to selling just one company's products.

You can sell products from your home, teach classes, hold crops, and market your business any way you choose. Hire yourself out to scrapbook, craft and photo stores, providing their customers with individual instruction and advice. Use your resale permit to participate in group buys and build your inventory from wholesale suppliers described in Chapter 4.

Tips for Success

Consulting can be a very satisfying way to stay involved in scrapbooking, help others preserve their memories, and make money while you're at it.

Creative Consulting

Julie Southwick of Scrappin' for Fun designs and creates theme kits of coordinated papers, stickers, and die-cuts. The kits are easy to use; customers just pick a theme and add their own photos. Julie sells her kits at craft fairs, crops, trade shows, and her local scrapbooking store. Contact Julie at (402) 421-8302 or crop101@aol.com.

Whether you devote a few hours a month or consult full time, the following tips will steer you toward success.

Create Your Own Markets

Drum up business by finding ways to add value to your local craft or scrapbooking stores. Teach their classes, create albums for others, or sell them custom kits of coordinated materials to supplement their product inventory.

- Give customers personal attention they just can't get anywhere else.

- Be friendly, courteous, and professional. If a customer asks a question for which you have no answer, research the issue and promptly call back with a reply.

- Actively market your business and build customer loyalty. Find ways to keep previous customers informed and interested. Publish a newsletter with product announcements and ideas. Invite customers to your "10-pages-a-week" club, Tuesday morning crops, "Mom's Night Out," or "Real Men Scrap."

- Set aside a time each week to do paperwork, marketing, ordering, and inventory management. Find a couple of hours while the kids take their naps, do homework, or head off to the park with Grandma or Dad.

Survey Says!

- Skills consultants wished they'd known more about before beginning their businesses:
  Financial issues: 24%
  Advertising and marketing: 21%
  General business skills: 18%
  Scrapbooking products, tools, and techniques: 11%
  Time management: 17%
  People skills: 6%
  Stress management: 3%

- Maintain accurate records. A simple accounting of your purchases and sales is far better than none at all.

- Don't forget to scrap! Take time to keep up on your craft and enjoy the simple pleasure scrapping brings to your day.

- Network, network, network. Stay in touch with other scrappers and consultants. Share ideas and stay motivated.

Survey Says!

- Amount of time consultants spend working on their own scrapbooks since starting their business:
  Less time: 37%
  Same amount of time: 37%
  More time: 23%

More Consultant Resources

Software
Instructor is designed for consultants to track customer information, sales, expenses and inventory. Try before you buy: download and use it for up to 30 days with no charge. See www.scrapsoft.com

On the Internet
There are many online sites and e-mail lists specifically for consultants, including:

- Creative Memories consultants: From groups.yahoo.com, subscribe to CMCarchive, Hobbycmc, CM-Handouts, CMCfriends, CM-letters-kit-ideas, and Scrappinthecmway

- All consultants: From groups.yahoo.com, subscribe to Layouts, Scrapbusinesses, Cr8mcides, Scrapping, and 2scrapswap. Use the message boards at PictureTalk (www.dmarie.com)

Luck is a matter of preparation meeting opportunity—Oprah Winfrey

Chapter 8.
Commissioned Scrapbooker

Start-up cost:	Low
Income potential:	Low to moderate
Commitment:	Part-time or full-time
Financial risk:	Low

Do friends and family ooh and aahhh over your scrapbook creations and say you should be in business? Would you rather create pages than sell products or teach classes? If you answered "yes" to both, then becoming a commissioned scrapbooker—a fancy term for someone who creates albums for others—may be the perfect business for you. Combine a timesaving service with a creative way to preserve photos and memories, and you've got a dynamic business opportunity.

Where to Start

Here's what you need to know before getting started as a scrapper-for-hire.

Expertise. How well do you know your craft? Are you a newcomer to scrapbooking or a master of many techniques? You don't have to be the best or most creative scrapbooker in the world to scrap for others, but you should at least be able to skillfully design and complete basic page layouts. (How would you feel about having your car repaired by someone who *wants* to be a mechanic, but doesn't know how to change the oil?)

Learn how to coordinate colors to set tone, create harmony, and develop contrast on a page. Improve your lettering ability. As you become more experienced, you can enhance your repertoire—and charge more for specialty items like embossing, paper-piecing, specialty borders, and working with vellum.

Keep improving your skills. Study scrapbooking magazines, including *Creating Keepsakes*, *Memory Makers, Paper Kuts,* and *Ivy Cottage Creations* to learn new trends and techniques. Attend classes, crops, and expos to keep up on products and ideas. Challenge yourself by entering layout contests at your local scrapbooking store, on your favorite website, and in magazines. Find ways to work more efficiently and complete more pages in less time. As your experience grows, so will your professional piggy bank.

Define your style. Decide whether you'll specialize in one particular style or many. Do you favor simple, uncluttered pages with bold borders and simple photo matting? Do you like to do lots of journaling, or only include titles and captions? Perhaps your forté is creating elegant wedding albums or Victorian pages with a soft, muted look.

Bragging Rights

How many total pages—both personal and commissioned—have you completed since you started scrapbooking? Keep a running tally, and advertise your vast experience on your business card and other promotional materials: "More than 300 pages completed!" Very impressive!

Will you create any type of album for customers, or do you prefer to focus on juvenile, heritage, pet or travel collections? If you don't fancy a particular theme or style, start by offering basic layouts. You'll develop a specific interest as your business progresses. Just be sure it's a specialty with enough demand to produce the profit you want.

Create a demonstration scrapbook. As a professional, you need a portfolio of your work to show prospective customers. What better way to showcase your creative abilities than showing a scrapbook of your best work? Design sample pages around the techniques and themes you offer. Vary pages to give customers an idea of what you can do with their photos. Use corner punches on some photos, and silhouette or double-mat others. Create bold titles and descriptive captions. Include the pages you've entered in contests and any awards you've received. Add photographs of each commissioned job you complete. Build an excellent visual record of your scrapbooking business.

Develop a process. Think through your entire process before meeting your first customer. Where will you meet? What information will clinch the sale? How much will you charge? How will you address customer questions and concerns? Read through the remainder of this chapter, particularly the sample customer contract. List the steps you need to complete from the time you first make contact with the customer to delivery of the completed album. Practice your entire process on a friend or family member, then revise it as necessary until you're comfortable with your comprehensive list of action steps.

Where To Find Customers

Just about everyone has photos. That means just about anyone is a potential client. Send a business card and announcement to everyone you know, starting with family, friends, and co-workers who already know and trust you and who appreciate your scrapbooking skill. Then expand your marketing to find new customers. You can approach new markets in two ways:

■ Look for customers who'll be interested in the type of albums you want to create. If you want to make wedding albums, place your business cards or brochures with bridal salons, photography studios, tuxedo rental shops, and wedding planners. Love to make pet albums? Target owners, stores, groomers, kennels, and veterinarians.

■ Develop album themes to appeal to a specific group of customers. Think how a specific business can benefit by having a scrapbook: nail and hair salons, child care providers, real estate agents, landscapers, gym owners, and medical professionals can use scrapbooks to promote their businesses. Use your local phone directory for inspiration; it's a gold mine of ideas.

Be alert to activities and events that are announced in your local news media. Offer to create a scrapbook of the town parade or the annual children's theater. Suggest that the Chamber of Commerce commemorate a local anniversary with a memory album. Participate in town fairs, craft malls, and church bazaars. Donate several free pages to a local auction, raffle, or benefit.

Sometimes timing is everything. Planting ideas to coincide with holidays and special occasions can bring in new business. Promote scrapbooks as gifts for birthdays, retirements, Mother's Day, Christmas, or bat and bar mitzvahs. Just think of the potential business from the high school prom or the school play. Leave flyers or business cards at your local craft, photo, and scrapbooking stores. With a bit of creative thinking, you can develop more ideas than you can use.

Thousands of Customers in One Place

If you have an amusement park or other tourist attraction nearby, you have a captive audience. Create sample pre-designed pages of the facility, in which visitors can insert their own photos. Then make an appointment to pitch your idea to the gift shop director or public relations manager.

The Internet is a treasure trove of customers just waiting to learn how your services can benefit them. Target specific groups (parents, moms, genealogists, etc.), then post to their message boards and chat rooms. List your website with search engines (read more on that in Chapter 6). Making albums for someone you won't be able to meet in person requires a few additional precautions. E-mail, snail mail, or fax samples of your work, then conduct a consultation by telephone.

You might even provide periodic updates to long-distance customers by scanning and e-mailing representative pages as they are completed. Strongly suggest your customers insure the photos and other materials they send to you, and do the same when you return the completed album (see the sample contract at the end of this chapter).

The Customer Consultation

Your consultation with the customer is an interactive session. She shows her photos and tells you what she has in mind. You show album samples, discuss techniques, and make helpful suggestions. Explain options for album size, themes, lettering styles, color selection, and layouts. Discuss your contract. Make sure she understands what you're providing, when you're providing it, and how much she'll be charged.

During the consultation, determine what your customer wants. (Customers who are unfamiliar with scrapbooking may not know what they want beyond getting all their photos organized and into albums.) Does she prefer to have photos organized chronologically, by theme, date, or subject? Is she partial to certain colors or a particular style?

Encourage Customers to Spread the Word

No promotional tool is more powerful than word-of-mouth endorsements from satisfied customers.

⊙ Promote your business every time customers show off their custom albums. Mount a small label to the inside back cover: *"This album was created especially for you by Memories from the Heart (203-899-9999)."* Or use a rubber stamp for this purpose. Hero Arts (www.heroarts.com), for example, sells a "Created by _____" stamp.

⊙ Encourage referrals. Give each customer several business cards with their name written on the back. Each time you get a referral with one of the cards, reward the original customer with a discount on her next project.

Will she provide photo captions or add them herself? Does she want you to leave space on each page for her own journaling? Ask customers to first sort their photos, lightly number each one on the back with a photomarking pen, and list any special information or instructions on a corresponding inventory list, as shown on the sample below.

Play It Safe

Explain how photos are cropped and discuss options for mounting. Ask your customer to identify any of her photos that should not be cropped or permanently mounted.

Add any other inventory items you think necessary, but make the inventory list as easy as possible— you don't want to overwhelm or discourage the customer from going ahead with the project!

Set a time limit for your consultation. Provide a 45-to-60 minute meeting at no charge (many professionals provide free estimates), with any additional time charged at your hourly rate. Or require a modest consultation fee to cover your time.

Photo	Caption	OK to Crop?	Perm. Mounting?
1.			
2.			
3.			
4.			

↓

Other materials provided by customer:
1. 20 page protectors
2.
3.

↓

Emphasize Value!

Promote your business as a way customers can:

● Get their photos out of the closet and into albums.

● Replace old photo albums with archival-quality products.

● Complete their unfinished scrapbooks.

How Much Should You Charge?

As a commissioned scrapbooker, you're a professional providing a service based on expertise, like a personal trainer or a financial advisor. You want to make a reasonable profit without losing money or scaring potential customers away. Market demographics and economics impact your fee structure. You can probably charge more in upscale, metropolitan areas where the economy is strong than in areas where unemployment is higher and disposable income is considerably less. It may be tougher to sell your services where scrapbooking is still relatively unknown. You can turn that to your advantage, however, with some clever marketing.

Barter and Swap

Why not trade services with customers? You create their albums in exchange for ironing, gardening, or babysitting. Offer to develop an album for your accountant (or other professional) in return for his services.

There are four ways to structure your charges:

- by the hour
- by the photo
- by the page (a single side)
- by the project

No matter which option you choose, the formula to determine your profit is the same:

$$Labor + Cost\ of\ materials = Total\ customer\ charge$$

Your profit is built into the labor component, which represents the value of your time. For example, you might charge $10 per hour, $1 per photo, or $5 per page, plus the actual cost of materials you use; or you can apply an overall rate that includes your labor and materials.

Many customers don't understand how much work and time it takes to create scrapbook pages, so it's difficult for them to value a job charged by the hour or entire project. Both methods require you to estimate the overall project, as does charging by the photo. Charging by the page is a sensible alternative for both you and the customer. Explain the various tasks involved in creating a page—designing the overall layout, cropping and matting photos, creating borders, and lettering—to help customers understand the skill and time required.

Survey Says!

- How commissioned scrapbookers structure their charges:
  By the page: 46%
  By the project: 41%
  By the hour: 12%

Here's how to calculate an average price per page:

1. Determine your hourly rate.

a) How much your time is worth? $10, $15, or $20 an hour? First decide on a reasonable, profitable hourly rate.

b) Working at a comfortable pace, count the number of pages you can make in an hour. Use the same type of materials and layouts you'll offer customers. This will determine your average page-per-hour.

c) Divide #a by #b to determine your price per page. If your hourly rate is $10 and you can consistently complete two pages an hour, your charge per page is $5. Here are three examples of this pricing structure:

Hourly rate	Charge per page (2 pages/hour)	Charge per page (3 pages/hour)
$10.00	$ 5.00	$3.35*
$15.00	$ 7.50	$5.00
$20.00	$10.00	$6.70*

* rounded up to the nearest nickel

2. Decide how you'll charge for materials. In addition to your labor, you should recoup the cost of materials. To do so, either *add* this cost to your per-page rate (Example #1) or *include* this cost in your per-page rate (Example #2).

Example #1: $5 per page plus the actual cost of materials used.

Example #2: $7.50 per page, which includes all materials used.

To use the second method, determine the cost of materials for an average page, as shown in the following example.

Item per page	Cost per item
1 12" x 12" page	$ .40
1 page protector	.45
3 stickers	.60
1 die-cut	.30
3 photo mounts	.30
2 mats in contrasting colors	.45
Total (average) per page	$2.50

An alternative method of charging is to offer a tiered-rate schedule depending on the complexity of the page layouts, for example:

- $8.00 per page for basic, quick layouts.

- $10.00 per page for basic layouts with double photo matting, special borders, and hand-lettered titles.

- $12.00 per page for paper-piecing, Coluzzle, embossing, and other special techniques.

List conditions for which you'll charge more or less than your standard rates. Increase rates for businesses or labor-intensive projects. Charge your hourly rate to customers who provide their own materials. Offer discounts to first-time customers, seniors, and customers who refer others to you. Offer to complete a free page for every 10 or 12 pages ordered.

Should You Profit from Materials?

At a minimum, incorporate the actual cost of materials into your price calculations. If you purchase materials at wholesale cost, either add a small markup, or pass the savings along to the customer as a way of keeping your rates affordable.

Stay on Schedule

Complete projects on time without undue stress by breaking them into manageable increments. Work backwards from your project's due date to determine how many pages you need to complete per day: You need to complete three pages a day to deliver a 42-page project in two weeks (42 total pages ÷ 14 days = 3 pages per day).

More Issues About Fees

Here are a few additional issues to consider when structuring your charges:

■ Consider placing a limit on the number of pages you take on as a single project. Scrapping years of accumulated photos may be overwhelming for you and cost-prohibitive for the customer.

■ Emphasize the value of your service. In addition to your expertise (as evidenced by your beautiful sample work), provide free pickup and delivery, and free or low-cost consultation. Most importantly, you're preserving precious family memories that will be enjoyed by generations to come.

■ Decide what your "redo" policy will be if a customer is dissatisfied with a page or an entire project.

When You Raise Your Rates

Notify prior customers with a postcard suggesting they schedule new projects before the new rates take effect. Or honor old rates for prior customers and charge only new customers the higher rates.

■ Require a 25-50% down payment before you begin a project.

Nice Touches

A little bit of thoughtfulness goes a long way. Customers will appreciate and remember extra efforts to show you value their patronage.

■ If customers will be adding their own journaling, provide an acid-free pen with each completed album.

■ Provide a coupon for a small discount on future services.

■ If the customer is having the album made for someone else, include a small gift card with the finished product.

The Customer Contract

Always sign a contract with the customer *before* beginning a job. Your contract should clarify, in plain language, the terms of your service and the responsibilities of both parties. The contract, or customer agreement, can help to avoid misunderstandings, potential legal problems, and loss of future business. It also serves as a handy checklist of the most important issues you need to discuss during the consultation.

Christina Hrudka and her sister Nicole Shue use the contract shown on the following three pages for their business, Scrappin' Sisters.

Avoid Contract Mumbo Jumbo

Your contract should clarify the agreements between you and your customer, so develop a document that can be easily understood. Use simple and concise statements. Opt for everyday English and grammar. Avoid legalese like "wheretofore," "heretofore," and "the part of the first part."

To ensure the terms and conditions of their contract are read and understood, Christina and Nicole ask their customers to initial each clause.

Scrappin' Sisters

361 Dolphin Drive
Oceanside, CA 92045
(760) 430-0508
scrappin_sisters@hotmail.com

Consultant-Customer Agreement

Date_____Customer Name_____
Address_____
Phone_____E-mail_____
Preferred hours/method of contact_____
Type, size, color, and number of albums requested_____
Date of completion_____Cost of project_____
Delivery method_____
Supplies provided by customer_____
Other information_____

Please read the following provisions carefully, initialing each and signing the Agreement in its entirety.

1. All items to be included in the scrapbook (photographs, memorabilia, etc., are to be mounted in the scrapbook using only photo-safe adhesives, papers, accents, pens, etc. I understand only those products labeled by reputable companies as "archival quality" or "photo safe" will be used, and thus any resulting damage from defective products is not the liability of Scrappin' Sisters. *initials_____*

2. Scrappin' Sisters is only responsible for the photos and memorabilia listed on the signed and attached Inventory sheet. In the event photos and/or memorabilia provided are damaged by fire, flood, earthquake, hurricane, tornado, or other unavoidable disaster (including, but not limited to, theft or auto accident) while in our possession, Scrappin' Sisters is only liable for the cost of reprinting photos from negatives. I understand irreplaceable photographs and memorabilia will not

Consultant-Customer Agreement (continued)

be knowingly accepted by Scrappin' Sisters for placement in the scrapbook. In the event irreplaceable photos or memorabilia are damaged, I accept full responsibility for their loss, and agree not to hold Scrappin' Sisters liable. *initials*_____

3. Unless otherwise specified, photos and memorabilia will be mounted in the album using photo-safe adhesives that are essentially considered permanent. While it may be possible to remove photos, it is not recommended as damage to the photos will likely occur. Any items I do not want to be permanently mounted are indicated on the attached Inventory sheet. *initials*_____

4. Photos and memorabilia specified for nonpermanent mounting will be placed in the album with photo-safe corners, allowing for easy and safe removal at a later date. *initials*_____

5. Unless otherwise specified, photos and memorabilia may be cut ("cropped") or altered during the creative process. Any items I do not want to be cut or altered are indicated on the attached Inventory sheet. *initials*_____

6. Scrappin' Sisters requires a deposit of 50% of the project cost at the time this Agreement is signed. For this specific project the deposit is $___. This deposit is nonrefundable and will be applied towards the purchase of the album and supplies needed to complete this project. A receipt will be provided. *initials*_____

7. When the album is completed, I understand I will be notified and the remaining 50% of the project cost will be due at the time the completed album is picked up. For this project the remaining balance is $___. If the delivery method specified in this Agreement is not "in person," the balance will be due 7 days after confirmation of delivery. Any unused photos or memorabilia will be returned with the completed album. *initials*_____

8. If the delivery method specified in this Agreement is "shipped," Scrappin' Sisters will send the album through a reputable mailing service (the United States Post Office, United Parcel Service, or Federal Express). I understand the cost of this project includes a fee for shipping and handling. Scrappin' Sisters will send the album registered and insured for the cost of the project, with proof of delivery required. I understand Scrappin' Sisters is only responsible for the shipping insurance, and the shipping agent will be liable in the event an album is lost or damaged during shipping. *initials*_____

9. If the delivery method desired changes from "in person" to "shipped" after this Agreement is signed, a signed addendum to this Agreement will be made.

Consultant-Customer Agreement (continued)

The amount of shipping and handling charges will depend on the size of this project. I understand the additional fee for shipping and handling will be due PRIOR to the album being shipped. *initials_____*

10. Acceptance of the completed album is construed as acceptance of and satisfaction with all work completed. In the event an album is shipped to me and I am not satisfied, I understand I may return the album within 7 days from the initial confirmation of receipt so that Scrappin' Sisters may make my specified adjustments. I understand I am solely responsible for insuring and returning the album to Scrappin' Sisters. Upon completion of the adjustments, Scrappin' Sisters will resend the completed album registered and insured for the cost of the project, with proof of delivery required. *initials____*

11. Every effort will be made by Scrappin' Sisters to complete this project on time. If the album is not finished by the date specified in this Agreement, Scrappin' Sisters will deduct 20% of the total cost from the final balance due. *initials ___*

12. Please initial one:

I authorize Scrappin' Sisters to make and keep copies of any album pages created for me. I understand these copies may be used by Scrappin' Sisters for advertisement purposes. *intials___*
                    or
I do not authorize Scrappin' Sisters to make and keep copies of any album pages created for me. *initials ___*

13. All returned checks will be subject to a $25 fee. Returned checks not made good by cash or money order within 7 days will be forwarded to the proper authorities. *initials_____*

As a client of Scrappin' Sisters, I understand and agree to the provisions of this contract. By my signature, I indicate my willingness to abide by the provisions contained herein.

Customer Signature_____Date_____

Scrappin' Sisters
Consultant Signature_____Date_____
                    Christina Hrudka or Nicole Shue

Three Ways to Control Inventory Costs

Avid scrapbookers often find it difficult to curb their spending habits. You buy a few papers here and some tools there, and before you know it, you have products piled up everywhere. The problem with an out-of-control inventory is the investment required. The more overhead you have, the less money you have on hand...and the greater the stress is to recoup that investment. Here are a few tips for keeping your inventory costs in line:

1. **Curb the impulse to buy.** Exercise control over your scrap addiction! Create a monthly purchasing budget and stick to it. Keep samples of basic items to show customers. Invest in basic tools and products you need for every project: rulers, scissors, cutters, adhesives, and templates.

2. **Buy materials with the customer's deposit.** Use each customer's down payment to fund individual projects.

3. **Buy more for less.** Stock up on materials during sales and discounts. Buy products from wholesale suppliers. Participate in group buys. Ask your local scrapbooking store manager if you can tag onto her orders— she may be amenable to this arrangement if she doesn't consider you to be competition. See Chapter 4, *The Home Store,* for more ideas about managing inventory.

More Commissioned Scrapbooker Resources

Publications and Books
There are so many good scrapbook magazines and idea books for layouts, ideas, techniques, and other helpful information. See your local craft, hobby, bookstore, or scrapbooking stores.

On the Internet
- Find lots of books and software on the Internet. Try dMarie (www.dmarie.com), *Creating Keepsakes* (www.creatingkeepsakes.com), Cut 'N' Fun (www.cutnfun.com), or your favorite online store

- Several online message boards and e-mail groups schedule group buys,

On the Internet (continued)

offer support and ideas, and discuss making scrapbooks for others: Scrapping4others (subscribe at groups.yahoo.com) is an informative and supportive group that offers practical advice about marketing strategies, pricing, product and layout tips, and the nuts and bolts of running your business. It's also an excellent source for group buys

■ Log on to groups.yahoo.com and subscribe to discussion lists that catch your fancy

■ Use the resources listed in other chapters for more ideas about page layouts, finding customers, and scrapbooking techniques

A master can tell you what he expects of you. A teacher, though, awakens your own expectations.—Patricia Neal

Chapter 9.
Teacher

Start-up cost:	Low
Income potential:	Low
Commitment:	Low to moderate
Financial risk:	Low

Teaching is a labor of love. For those who have the inclination, there's nothing more satisfying than sharing enthusiasm and expertise with others. Just think of it: each class you teach may inspire others to preserve their memories.

Brush Up on Your Skills

Think back to your school days. Why did you enjoy your favorite teachers so much? Probably because they knew their topics well, communicated with gusto and made learning fun. Strive to be that kind of teacher—the one who is surrounded by students long after class is over. Provide a positive experience to empower your students with confidence and creativity.

Show and Tell

Actions speak louder than words. Always show samples and demonstrate techniques.

You need two basic skills before you begin teaching: expertise regarding your topics and teaching skills. One or the other isn't enough. You need both to be the kind of teacher who will keep students coming back for more. Take classes yourself as you constantly strive to improve your abilities. Assess what works and what doesn't. Observe the techniques of other teachers, and join online chat groups to learn more about teaching techniques and communication skills.

What Should You Teach?

Teaching presents endless opportunities. Start your repertoire with one or two classes, then expand your offerings as you increase and improve your scrapbooking and teaching abilities. Read scrapbooking magazines. Regularly visit favorite scrapbooking websites to keep up on new products, trends, terms, and techniques. Here are a few ideas for classes.

Just the basics. Scrapbooking can be overwhelming to the novice. Why not conduct an Introduction to Scrapbooking class, where you simply discuss terminology and demonstrate basic products? Describe different types of adhesives, albums, page protectors, and scissors. Unravel the mysteries of archival products. Explain the advantages and disadvantages of webhinge, postbound, three-ring, and other albums. Show how to use shapes and colors to design basic page layouts. Give pointers on organizing photo collections, journaling, and scrapping on a budget. Help novice and experienced scrapbookers with creative ways to journal.

Techniques. Consider classes on lettering, borders, rubber stamping, cropping, punch art, and other ways to improve scrapbooking skills and enhance pages.

Go Straight to the Source

Many product manufacturers provide free handouts and teaching aids for their products. Contact various companies or visit their websites.

Show time-saving methods to create pages quickly. Attract experienced scrappers with new techniques: quilt pages, pocket pages, paper folding, and photo tinting. Give classes on creating fancy pages using lace borders, ribbons, vellum, crimped or embossed papers, or other specialty items. Show how to use new products, and innovative ways to use old products.

Theme albums. Be alert to popular trends and themes. Show students how to make ABC albums, or create page layouts with baby, heritage, Disney or pet themes. Show how to put together recipe pages and cookbook albums (*Meals and Memories: How To Create Keepsake Cookbooks* shows how. Contact (800) 431-1579 or see www.carlopress.com). Give ideas for scrapping everyday occurrences and unusual happenings. Schedule classes to create albums for holidays, unique events and special occasions.

Where to Find Customers

Target existing scrappers and newcomers. Leave business cards and flyers at your local scrapbook, photo, and craft stores. Contact operators of scrapbooking expos, conventions, and trade shows to find out how you can teach classes during their events.

Look in your phone directory under "Associations" and brainstorm how you might appeal to different groups. Design classes for seniors, teens and parents. Teach a private class for the quilting guild, the bowling league, and the genealogy club. Approach the activities coordinator of your church group, scouting troop and summer camp. Dazzle Little League moms with your sample pages, and propose a class to show them how to make their own special sports albums with their little darlings as the star attractions.

Coordinate a weekly crop, swap or coffee klatch at which you teach a new technique. Teach a basic scrapbooking class at your community college or adult education facility.

Ahoy There, Matey!

Expand your promotional ideas to include the unconventional. Cruise lines are always interested in teachers who can provide interesting classroom ideas and activities while at sea. Approach activity directors with an excellent proposal, classroom outlines, and your sample portfolio.

Identify your potential customer base. Consider where they are, how to reach them, then develop promotional materials to appeal to the specific group you're targeting.

Teach at Scrapbook Stores: A Win-win Situation

One of the most logical and lucrative places to teach is your local scrapbook store. Approach the opportunity with the store manager or owner as a mutually beneficial relationship. Call first to ask for an appointment. Be prepared to wow her with your incredible scrapbooking skills (of course, you'll have your portfolio of samples with you), and show how you'll add value to her store. If she already has a class schedule, propose different classes, or out-of-hours and weekend workshops.

Provide class outlines, references, and positive evaluations from previous students. Point out the benefits of having you teach in her store:

■ Your classes will bring new customers and new business into her store.

■ Customers are more likely to buy more products when they know how to use them properly and creatively.

■ Classes and workshops will provide another source of store income.

■ If the owner is already teaching classes, hiring you will allow her to spend her time on other priorities.

If the store doesn't have adequate classroom area, you can still create a win-win situation. Ask if you may place your business cards or brochures in the store to promote your classes in another location. Provide your class schedule so it can be included in the store newsletter or website. In turn, you'll refer students to the store to buy their class materials.

How to Charge for Classes

If you plan to provide students with classroom materials, either include the materials in the price of the class, or charge a flat fee for the class and something extra for materials. If you want students to bring materials to class, let them know when they register.

Compare charges for similar classes in the area. If there aren't any available, check craft and hobby classes and adjust your prices appropriately. If you'll be teaching in scrapbook stores, discuss with the owner whether store employees will collect classroom fees at the time of registration (in the store), or if you'll collect fees during class. Store owners may have their own ideas about how you'll be compensated. The two of you might split class revenues according to a mutually agreed-upon percentage, or she may pay you a flat fee or percentage for each student who attends.

A Portable Business

When Cynthia Anning's husband was transferred to the Naval Air Station in Keflavik, Iceland, she discovered scrapbooking and found a teaching business. The local scrapbook instructor was returning to the U.S. and Cynthia stepped in to fill the teaching void. Now she conducts scrap-booking and archival safety workshops and holds special crop parties on the base. Besides doing something she loves, Cynthia has a business she can pack up and take with her wherever she relocates. Check her Cre-ative Scrapbooking website (www.creativescrapbooking.com) for ideas and layouts.

It's always a good idea to have a written contract describing the terms of your teaching agreement, including how you'll to be compensated and any discount you'll be given on scrapbooking materials.

Six Tips for Better Classes

Your classes will go smoothly if you're well prepared. Once you've taught a few, preparation becomes second-nature.

1. **Be prepared.** It's disappointing and frustrating to take a class from a teacher who is unprepared or forgets half of her materials. Prepare well to make your class a success. Know your subject. Try a dry run with friends before you teach a paying audience. Create your class outline, samples, and student kits in advance.

2. **Start with an icebreaker.** Some people are intimidated by a classroom environment. Before you dive into your class subject, take a few moments to break the ice and make your students feel comfortable. Describe your background and what attendees can expect to learn. Ask everyone to briefly introduce themselves, say why they're attending, and how long they've been scrapping. Tell an amusing anecdote. Set an informal mood. Don't be afraid to have fun!

3. **Provide handouts.** Students may not remember a lettering technique or how to make a border when they get around to trying it at home. Provide simple, concise handouts to reinforce classroom lessons.

4. **Use hands-on teaching techniques.** People learn by doing. Demonstrate how to use a Border Buddy, letter a title, or a create a paper-piecing pattern, then have the students try it on their own.

5. **Be ready to deal with "interesting" personalities.** Not every one learns at the same pace.

A Little One-on-one is Always Nice

Walk around the room while students are working on their pages. Answer individual questions and help those who are struggling with techniques or design ideas.

Allow ample time to answer questions. And, let's face it, there's one in every class: Ms. "I-Have-Nothing-To-Journal," Miss "Would-You-Repeat-That-Again (and again, and again)?" and the all-time favorite of teachers everywhere, Madame "That's-Not-How-I-Do-It!" Unless someone is absolutely disruptive, smile and be patient.

6. **Ask for feedback.** Use evaluations as the benchmark of your proficiency. Design a quick and simple evaluation form and ask all your students to complete it before they leave class. Ask them to rate their overall satisfaction with the class content, whether it lived up to its promotion, how it might be improved, if they feel they can duplicate class techniques on their own, and your teaching style and abilities. Do a little research while you're at it: ask students to list future classes they would like to attend.

Stuck for an Idea?

Stuck on the Edge is an excellent monthly color publication for creating borders using Mrs. Grossman's stickers. Each issue includes color photos, easy-to-follow instructions, and supply lists for 11 to 14 original designs. Subscribe by calling (612) 861-4814 or visiting www.stuckontheedge.com.

More Teacher Resources

On the Internet

- Log on to groups.yahoo.com and subscribe to teachingsb, scrapteachers, and sbhandouts

- Hot Off the Press (www.craftpizazz.com) has lots of ideas, information and layouts for teachers

- *Creating Keepsakes* offers hundreds of fonts at the Lettering Delights website (www.letteringdelights.com)

Opportunities are usually disguised by hard work, so most people don't recognize them.—Ann Landers

Chapter 10.
Event Planner

Start-up cost:	Low to high
Income potential:	Low to high
Commitment:	Low to high
Financial risk:	Low to high

Are you creative and well-organized? Are you able to handle several details, tasks and responsibilities at once without becoming overly stressed? Do you excel at planning, decision-making and followthrough? If you answered yes to all of these questions, you might enjoy being a scrapbooking event planner, either for yourself or on behalf of local scrapbook stores or groups. The success of your events depends upon your ability to multitask. If participants are happy with the experience you provide, they'll rave about it to their friends, and return for your next event. If they have a dissatisfying experience, they're even more likely to tell their friends and you'll probably lose future business. You may also be faced with participants demanding refunds.

A Glossary of Events, Occasions, and Happenings

Scrapbooking events are popular and can be very profitable for the folks who coordinate them. The list of scrapbooking events continues to grow each year as more and more people jump to cash in on the industry's overwhelming popularity and success. Here's an introduction to different scrapbooking events.

Crops. A crop is an organized opportunity for participants to work on their scrapbooks together, make new friends, try new ideas and have a great time. Crops range from small neighborhood affairs to regional events with hundreds or thousands of participants. Consultants and retailers hold crops to sell products and encourage customers to scrap. Some crops include free use of die-cut machines, paper cutters, rubber stamps, rulers and other tools.

Schedule regular crops for participants to set aside time to work on their scrapbooks. Sponsor a Monday Night Football crop session or a mom's crop once a week while the kids are in school. Make it interesting. Provide door prizes and hold contests. Award a small prize for the cropper who uses more red on her pages or the one who completes the most pages during the session.

Flexible Hours

Kim Amond of Heirlooms from the Heart conveniently schedules crops for her customers. Participants at Kim's morning Sip 'n Scraps and evening Crop 'n Shops work on their pages, enjoy new friends, and order products from Kim's home store. Contact (315) 451-2781.

Encourage paper exchanges. You might charge a modest admission fee and provide kits of the same papers, die-cuts and stickers, and see who uses them most creatively. Include "grab bags" of punches, cardstock, pens and other items participants can trade with each other.

Getaways and retreats. These away-from-home, overnight scrapping events are held in bed-and-breakfast facilities, spas, hotels, campgrounds and resorts. To see just how popular these are, check the online annual event schedule at the websites listed at the end of this chapter. Many of the events sell out completely early in the year.

Profile: Scrapbookers Dream Vacations

Nancy and Dale Bohrer design weekend getaways especially for scrapbookers. In addition to meals and lodging at beautiful resorts, the price of admission to their Scrapbookers Dream Vacations includes the Cut-N-Punch Center, where croppers have free use of die-cut machines, scissors, cutters, crimpers, lightboxes, templates, a plethora of other supplies and tools and unlimited cropping hours. Some participants have been known to crop through the night! Contact Dream Events at (877) 321-9054 or www.dreameventsinc.com.

Expos, shows, and conventions. These are larger events held in convention centers and at fairgrounds, often with hundreds or thousands of scrapbooking enthusiasts. Participants can attend crops, take classes, and hear well-known guest speakers. Rows of vendor booths line the aisles, where participants can examine and buy the newest products. The key to successful large events is good planning and great marketing. Use the listings at www.scraplink.com to get the latest information on the what, where and when of major scrapbook happenings.

Trade shows. These business-to-business expos and conventions are open only to the trade. A reseller's permit, business license or other proof of your business is usually required for entry.

Come Prepared!

You must show proof of business ownership to gain entry to a trade show (business cards are usually not accepted). Contact show sponsors for a list of acceptable documents.

Manufacturers introduce new products, giving retailers an opportunity to try before they buy. The largest scrapbooking trade shows are those sponsored annually by Memory Trends, the Hobby Industry Association (HIA) and the Association of Crafts and Creative Industries (ACCI). See *More Event Resources* in this chapter for contact information.

How to Get Started

Learn the ropes. The best way to learn is by doing. Attend as many events as possible to observe and learn. Notice what works well and what doesn't. See how the pros handle pre-event publicity, registration, marketing, activity scheduling and other activities. Contact local event coordinators and ask to work for them in some capacity. If this isn't possible, help coordinate a local event for your school, church or association. The event may not be the same, but the overall learning experience will be valuable.

Start small. Profit and risk are proportionate to the size of your event. The bigger the event, the greater the responsibility, coordination and risk. Master small-scale events before moving on to bigger affairs.

Create theme events. Follow a popular theme to attract participants. Appeal to potential attendees with a chocolate-lovers crop (have plenty of goodies on hand), Mom's night out or a benefit for your favorite charity.

Scrap and Relax

Marjorie Kirchner of Main Street Memories in Pennsylvania provides scrapbooking retreats in a beautiful countryside setting. If the fishing, swimming and home cooking aren't enough to relax participants, the on-site masseuse will. Marjorie's annual three-day getaways feature a different theme each year, with door prizes, guest speakers and scavenger hunts. Best of all, plenty of time is devoted to what participants enjoy the most: working on their own scrapbooks. Contact (717) 867-4515 or MSMemreez@aol.com.

Offer value. Give participants their money's worth when they attend your event. Schedule scrap challenges, guest lecturers, silent auctions and product demonstrations by company representatives. Snacks or meals, if included, needn't be elaborate, but should be tasty.

Secure an adequate location. Always inspect your event space before locking in a date. Be sure the facility is large enough to accommodate all participants without being too crowded. Ensure adequate parking, dining and rest room facilities. If you're offering a getaway, look for B&Bs, resorts and hotels in beautiful, peaceful surroundings. Test the acoustics and address special needs, such as handicapped access or vegetarian

Honored Guests

Invite Becky Higgins or Lisa Bearnson of *Creating Keepsakes* magazine to your next crop or getaway. They often attend local scrapping events and include coverage of the event in the magazine. Contact (801) 224-8235.

diets. Some events are scheduled adjacent to popular tourist attractions, so Dad and the kids can hit the roller coasters or the beach while Mom crops all day.

Recruit experts. Product manufacturers, authors, and other experts are often available to conduct demonstrations, discuss new techniques, or sign books during your event. Call and invite them!

Secure exhibiting vendors. If you're going to ask vendors to participate in your event, be sure to send them information about scheduling, booth availability and pricing, and general information well in advance of notifying the public.

Ask for donations. Product manufacturers are often happy to donate a product or two for your goodie bags, contest awards, or door prizes. Don't be shy about asking. The worst you'll get is a refusal. If that happens, hopefully you'll have plenty of donations from other vendors who will come through for you.

Don't try to do everything yourself. Pulling off large events successfully requires lots of planning, coordination, organization, scheduling and double-checking. Recruit volunteers to help you.

First list everything that needs to be done, then assign tasks. Follow up to stay on schedule. Get together regularly to assess your progress and resolve any issues.

Scrap your success. Document each of your events with a scrapbook of photos, attendance records, overall sales, the type of classes you have and other data. You'll have a nice memento of your affair and a valuable marketing tool for future events.

Avoid Disaster

Consider limiting participants. Keep track of registrations so you won't have more people than you can handle. Use sellouts as a promotional tool; when promoting your next even, let people know they should reserve space in advance before you sell out (as the last event did).

Make a site visit. Before you sign a contract or give verbal agreement, take a trip to the event site. Ensure it's everything you need and expect before you hand over a deposit. And don't put up a non-refundable deposit if you don't think you can attract enough scrappers to recoup your costs.

Provide value. Strive to provide a great overall experience for attendees. Lines that are too long, classes that don't deliver on promises, or poor-quality activities may not offset other positive aspects of your events. Attend to every detail from preregistration to closing time. If participants will arrive from different areas, try to arrange special discounted rates with airlines, car rental agencies and nearby hotels, or engage one travel agent to handle all reservations.

Plan appealing events that are instructive and fun and deliver on what you promise. Delight participants with quality activities, useful information or a surprise lunchtime speaker or workshop instructor.

Have a backup plan. Sooner or later, Murphy's Law is bound to strike. Hopefully, it will be a slight mishap instead of a catastrophe: a scheduled instructor misses her flight or a product demonstrator comes down with the flu. Have a contingency plan in case something untoward occurs. Arrange for backup speakers or teachers who are willing to step in if needed.

Promote Your Event

Promote on a scale commensurate with the size of your event. If you're hosting a small event, invite scrappers you know or post a flyer in your local scrapbooking store. Market larger events broadly with a news release to the media and articles for scrapbooking newsletters. Post announcements on various websites, message boards and e-mail lists. Click on "Conventions" at Scraplink (www.scraplink.com) and post your information on each site listed. Emphasize the positive without promising anything you can't or won't provide.

More Event Planner Resources

Books
■ *How to Put on a Great Conference: A Straightforward, Friendly and Practical Guide* by Tom McMahon

■ *How to Develop and Promote Successful Seminars and Workshops: The Definitive Guide to Creating and Marketing Seminars, Workshops, Classes, and Conferences* by Howard L. Shenson

On the Internet
■ Check Creating Keepsakes (www.creatingkeepsakes.com) and Scraplink (www.scraplink.com) for listings of expos, conventions, getaways and other scrapbooking events

■ See Chapter 11 for information about trade shows

Shoot for the moon. Even if you miss, you'll land among the stars.
—Les Brown

Chapter 11.
Product Designer/ Developer

Start-up cost:	Moderate to high
Income potential:	Moderate to high
Commitment:	Part-time or full-time
Financial risk:	Moderate to high

Dramatic growth in the scrapbooking industry is feeding an almost insatiable demand for new products. Enterprising scrappers profit from new ideas every month. Just notice the growing number of product advertisements and frequent new product reviews featured in scrapbooking magazines and on websites.

You don't have to be a multimillion dollar corporation to successfully introduce a new product. In fact, many successful products have been launched from grassroots efforts by scrappers just like you. Maybe you have a background in graphic design, a yen to be a wholesaler, or your own scrapping has inspired an idea for a product you know others will appreciate and buy.

To profit from a successful product, you first need to make sure there's a market for your idea, develop it well and cost effectively, and then market it to wholesale and/or retail buyers. Some products are easier to develop and market than others. It may take less time and investment, for example, to get your line of background papers or stickers to market, than to develop a new tool which must be machined to precise specifications.

Shaping Profits

Stay-at-home mom Delisa Curran wasn't looking for a business when she was scrapping one day in 1997 with her friend Lisa Crabill. Frustrated with her handcut ovals, Delisa called several manufacturers and suggested an oval cutter would be a very popular product. Not one manufacturer thought it was a feasible idea. So Lisa asked her brother-in-law, Mark, an engineer and inventor, if he could produce a tool to cut perfect oval shapes. Two weeks later, Mark proudly produced a heavy steel cutter. Delisa and Lisa knew they had a winner. Mark's prototype proved an oval cutter was possible. Delisa, her husband, Lisa, and Mark formed a partnership and established Shaping Memories™.

The foursome first listed their goals (keep their day jobs and have no financial risk), and characteristics the product needed in order to succeed. Infused with $3,000 from Delisa's father-in-law, Mark began producing parts for a more refined and compact cutter, and the partners hired an attorney to file their patent. After lots of hard work and learning, the group had their first batch of the Oval Cropper™. Just one ad in *Memory Makers* started the phones ringing as orders began pouring in. In less than three years, the group sold more than 50,000 retail and wholesale units. Delisa, who spent 50 hours a week running the business, advises: "Prototypes often cost thousands of dollars. Find a manufacturer who shares your excitement and consider making him your partner." (Note: The Shaping Memories™ OvalCropper™ is now part of the Fiskars Consumer Products family.)

From Concept to Reality

How many times have you seen a new product and thought, "I could have done that!" The difference is that you didn't and the product designer did. Many of the wonderful tools we take for granted are the results of scrappers who got tired of saying, "Someone should produce a such-and-such," and then acted on their hunch. We all have ideas we think others would pay for, but few of us act upon our brainstorms.

There's more to developing a product than you might think. If you have a notion for a marketable product, you can try to sell it to an existing company or pursue it yourself. If you sell your idea outright, you have none of the headaches of marketing, manufacturing or distributing your product. You'll receive a lump-sum payment in exchange for all rights to the product. In some cases, you may negotiate instead for royalties on future sales. Here's a simplified summary of the idea-to-sales process.

Start with a great idea. Do you have an idea for a product that will improve, simplify or enhance some aspect of scrapbooking? As early as possible, start an idea journal. Using dated entries, record your thoughts about the product, how it will be used, its dimensions, why you think it will be successful and any other thoughts you have about it. Include drawings. This early documentation may help to verify your claim to the product if your patent is ever challenged.

Biz-to-Biz

Consumers aren't the only ones who shop on the Internet. It's also a hot marketplace for business-to-business sales. 90% of companies surveyed planned to buy and sell on the Internet. Consider a website for your wholesale market.

Determine whether your product will sell. You know you have a good idea, but do others agree? And, more importantly, will they buy it? Before corporations invest in production, they often conduct focus groups to determine the viability of their ideas. You can simulate your own version of focus groups by testing the ideas with fellow scrappers and retail store owners. Conduct a telephone survey of local scrappers or post a survey online.

Without divulging too much of your specific plans, ask general questions to determine whether your product or service would interest potential buyers. Another method of gauging interest is to create a mock ad for your idea and test response with retailers and consumers.

A Very BIG Idea

Stephanie Rahmatulla was scrapping when she had a very BIG idea. Wouldn't it be easier and faster to complete page layouts if borders, corners and stickers were coordinated? And wouldn't it be nice to have stickers without the traditional white margins? From teaching scrappers and her own experience, Stephanie thought her idea might be a pretty good one. So she created 12 different sticker designs and whisked them to the 1999 HIA show in Dallas, where she and her products were an instant hit. Retailers couldn't wait to get the stickers into their stores. (Two of her images are shown on this book's cover and section pages.) With new orders in hand, Stephanie launched her company, me & my BIG ideas, from her dining room table. There she took orders by day and filled them at night from inventory stacked in her garage.

In just two months, Stephanie's growing business demanded more space. She moved to a 3,000-square-foot warehouse, where she now employs 10 people. Her product line blossomed to include 48 different stickers, including adorable little people, clever sayings and alphabets. The company also sells 30 paper designs and an idea book. Not one to rest on her laurels, Stephanie also has several new designs on the drawing board. In 1999, Stephanie's stickers were voted "Consumer's Choice" on Jangle.com. Today, her products are among the most popular, and retailers have a hard time keeping them on the shelves. This is an amazing success story nurtured from a single good idea, Stephanie's belief in her own ability and superb business skills. Contact (949) 589-4607 or www.meandmybigideas.com.

Develop a business plan. Before you spend any money on production, develop a business plan for your idea. Describe your product or service, the structure of your company and how you'll fund production. Include complete strategies for testing, producing, promoting and selling your product or service. Identify your customer base and clearly state how you will reach it. Don't neglect this step. A well-developed business plan will highlight strengths and weaknesses in your idea and provide a roadmap from conception to sales. Read more about business plans in Chapter 16.

Do You Need a Lawyer?

Researching and filing a patent can be a complex, time-consuming effort. Your application must include a thorough description of your product and explain why it's worthy of a patent. Weigh the advantages and disadvantages of hiring a patent attorney to do this for you. See the suggested do-it-yourself books at the end of this chapter.

Apply for a patent. If you don't find a similar product mentioned in scrapbook publications, Internet websites and product catalogs, conduct a patent search to see if someone else has beaten you to the punch. You can hire an attorney or professional patent searcher, or do it yourself by searching the U.S. Trade and Patent Office's (USPTO) database. Use the online database at www.uspto.gov or speak with a customer representative at (703) 308-HELP. The agency also has an automated question-and-answer line at (800) PTO-9199.

If no one has already patented your idea, retain a lawyer to file your patent, or do it yourself (see the resources at the end of this chapter). People often file patents for products which never see the light of day. If someone has already filed for your product idea, contact them to see if they have plans to pursue it. You may be able to buy the patent and move forward with your idea.

Build a prototype. If you have a design for stickers, stamps, background paper or some other relatively simple product, an established manufacturer may be able to easily create a master and develop a prototype for you. Developing products, tools and other hardware is more complex, and may require several manufacturing runs to get the kinks out of the design and produce a finished product. Ask for cost estimates before you sign any agreements.

Require all contacts to sign a nondisclosure agreement, which states they will not share your idea with anyone else.

Develop packaging. Whether you develop a product or service, you'll need to package it in a way that is attractive and alluring to potential buyers. Design flyers or brochures for your service, or contact a professional designer to create packaging for your product (look under "product packaging" in the telephone directory or on the Internet). Don't underestimate the value of great packaging. Do you buy products in plain wrappings that scream "CHEAP" or "AMATEUR" next to their competitors on the shelve? Probably not, and your potential customers, either wholesale and retail, won't either. It takes a great product (and marketing) to get those all-important resales, but it takes creative, attractive packing to make the initial sale. Many great products have failed because they were presented in unprofessional or unalluring packaging.

Sell your idea. With prototype in hand and patent pending, you're ready to convince wholesalers and store owners to buy your product. The best possible way to introduce your product to retail store owners, distributors and wholesalers is to show it at the annual trade shows listed in the previous chapter. These shows are *the* places to introduce new products. Exhibitor booths sell out early, so reserve your space well in advance of the show dates. Before shows, send product announcements (include your assigned booth number) to retailers, wholesalers and distributors, inviting them to stop by and see your new product. Of course, you can market a product without going to the show, but that will take a lot longer and cost more.

Contact (435) 586-1449 or www.scrapbookpremier.com to advertise your product in *Scrapbook Premier,* a product publication sent free each quarter to every retail scrapbook store in the U.S. If you plan to sell directly to consumers, consider scrapbook events, direct sales, and advertising to market your product. With a quality product, great marketing, and plenty of persistence, hopefully you'll take so many orders during the shows, your life will never be the same.

The rest of the story. With firm orders for your product, you're ready to manufacture in quantity. Arrange for packaging and shipping. Decide whether you're going to handle all orders yourself or work through a distributor. If you plan to sell directly to retail customers, show your product at consumer conventions and expos. Advertise in scrapbooking publications and online.

Calculate Your Costs and Profits

Use the following formula to estimate your total profit (sales - cost = profit):

1. Calculate total sales:

	_____ Wholesale units sold @ $____ each = $_____
plus	_____ Retail units sold @ $____ each = $_____
Total sales:	$_____

2. Calculate total costs:

_____ Design
_____ Market test
_____ Produce prototype(s)
_____ Patent, copyright, or trademark fees
_____ Develop/manufacture
_____ Package
_____ Market
_____ Distribute
_____ Other

Total cost $_____

3. Subtract #2 from #1 to determine your profit.

Protect Your Work

If your product is a piece of manufactured hardware, you need a patent to protect your idea from copycats. You may also need a trademark, service mark, and/or copyright to protect the way your express your company name, product

The Sincerest Form of Flattery?

According to copyright law, a unique idea cannot be copied, but it can be expressed in another way. You can't legally reproduce and sell Mrs. Grossman's teddy bear stickers, but you can create and sell your own line of little bear stickers.

name, or promotional phrase. Here's a summary of these additional types of legal protection:

■ A *copyright*, designated by the "©" symbol, protects written and illustrated material, including designs, images, text, and software. A copyright protects the way you express an idea, rather than the idea itself. Anyone can write a book about starting a scrapbook business, but they cannot legally reproduce this book or parts of it and sell it under another title. If you release a lettering CD or design a line of stickers, copyright your work so it may not be copied, reused, or resold without your permission.

Your work is automatically copyrighted when you create it. But it pays to file for an official copyright, in case the ownership of your work is challenged. Getting a copyright is a cinch compared to a patent. Contact the U.S. Copyright Office at (202) 707-9100 to request form TX or download it from the website at lcweb.loc.gov/copyright/forms.

How to Conduct a Copyright or Trademark Search

1. Hire a professional search organization. Look in your telephone directory under "trademark" or use keywords "copyright search" and "trademark search" to find Internet services like Trademark Express at (800) 776-0530 or www.tmexpress.com, and Mr. Trademark at (888) 235-0200 or www.mrtrademark.com.

2. Hire a US Copyright Office librarian to conduct a search for you. Contact (202) 707-3000.

3. Do it yourself. Contact (703) 306-2654 for the Patent and Trademark Depository Library branch nearest you, or use the USPTO's online database at www.uspto.gov. Log on to lcweb.loc.gov to search the U.S. Copyright Office's database. See the resources listed at the end of this chapter.

■ A *trademark* is a name, brand, symbol, logo, or design that distinguishes your product from others. Limited legal protection is acquired simply by using your trademark (as long as someone else isn't already using the same trademark).

Register your product's trademark with your Secretary of State's office to provide copyright protection within your state. Register with the USPTO to provide exclusive U.S. rights to your trademark. The "™" symbol indicates a trademark that is pending registration, while "®" represents a registered trademark. Frances Meyer, for example, is the only company who may legally use the following words in this exact order:

> Frances Meyer Inc.®
> The Scrapbook Leader™

■ A servicemark, or "SM" symbol, is a registered trademark used for a service, rather than a product.

More Product Designer / Developer Resources

Books and Publications
■ *The Inventor's Notebook* by Fred Grissom and David Pressman

■ *Patent It Yourself* by David Pressman

■ *Patent Searching Made Easy: How to Do Patent Searches on the Internet and in the Library* by David Hitchcock

■ *The Trademark Registration Kit: Quick & Legal* by attorneys Patricia Gima & Stephen Elias

On the Internet
■ List your product with online stores that feature new product reviews

■ Nolo Press (www.nolopress.com) provides legal information, publications, and forms that can be downloaded to your computer

Writing became such a process of discovery that I couldn't wait to get to work in the morning: I wanted to know what I was going to say.—Sharon O'Brien

Chapter 12.
Writer

Start-up cost:	Low
Commitment:	Low
Income potential:	Low to moderate
Financial risk:	Low

If you take satisfaction filling a blank page with inspiring, imaginative, or informative text, writing may be the perfect professional niche for you. Do you have a way with words? A snappy turn of phrase? A straightforward or clever style of communicating ideas? You can turn these characteristics into cash by composing and selling books, articles, poems, and journaling guides to scrappers.

So Many Opportunities, So Little Time

Contrary to popular belief, unless you have bestseller on your hands, you're not likely to get rich as a writer. Writing is a very satisfying pursuit, however, and can provide a steady stream of income if you approach it like a business.

Millions of people and thousands of publications are looking for written information. Know what the market needs, learn to write well, and promote, promote, promote.

The most common advice in publishing circles is "write what you know." You must be knowledgeable about your topic to write convincingly and accurately. If you're not an expert, interview those who are. Research thoroughly to write an informative or entertaining article. (One of the pleasant rewards of writing is the knowledge you gain through research.)

Whether you write on a part-time or full-time basis, you'll be successful if you give the market something it needs: new information or old information presented in an innovative way. Start locally. Write short pieces for your town newspaper, PTA, or scrapbooking store. As you gain experience, target magazines, online websites and newsletters. Or go for the gold. Write a book. Whatever venue you choose, many sources will pay for your writing.

■ **Newspapers.** Write an article about the growing trend of preserving memories. Interview scrappers and owners of scrapbooking businesses. Tell why scrapbooking is so enjoyable or describe how a monthly crop strengthens neighborhood relationships. Contact the paper and ask for the Lifestyles Editor. Pay is usually minimal.

■ **Consumer magazines.** Magazines are always looking for fresh ideas and stories. Although there are just a handful of scrapbooking magazines, many traditional consumer magazines may also welcome articles on scrapbooking.

How Does It Sound?

The most enjoyable writing is straightforward. Write simply and clearly, as though you were having a conversation with someone. Vary sentence length. Test your writing by reading it aloud or asking someone else to read and critique your work.

The trick is to give your article a particular focus or "slant." (See *How To Sell Magazines Articles* later in this chapter.) Pay may vary from just a complimentary copy of the publication with your printed article to several hundred dollars.

Think of different ways an article on scrapbooking might benefit a particular magazine's readers. *Parents* magazine may welcome a piece about involving kids in scrapbooking or creating baby albums. *Dog Fancy* might be very interested in an article describing how owners who show their pets can turn pooch photos and blue ribbons into beautiful albums.

First Impressions Count!

Always be prepared with a fully-developed idea and samples of your very best writing when you approach a publisher or editor. You may not get another chance.

■ **Trade journals.** Many of these publications for specific businesses and industries may welcome information about using scrapbooks as career portfolios and promotional tools. You're writing for entrepreneurs, so emphasize the value of scrapbooks to their business, rather than the mechanics of design or layouts. Describe how owners can create their own business scrapbooks, or how they can locate a commissioned scrapbooker. As a rule, trade magazines usually pay less than consumer magazines.

What's a "Clip?"

Anyone who hires you for a writing assignment will want to see your "clips," or copies of your previously published articles. As a new writer, focus on building a clip file, even if the job doesn't pay much or anything at all. Then you can tackle bigger and better-paying jobs.

■ **Newsletters.** Newsletters often pay little or nothing at all, but they are good practice and a way to add published pieces to your portfolio. Write for your local church, organization or scrapbooking store. Go online to find scrapbooking sites that regularly e-mail newsletters to subscribers (check the websites listed at Scraplink).

Or enter the newsletter business. Develop monthly or quarterly articles about the industry, trends, ideas for layouts and creative ways to use products. Include a question and answer column. Then market the newsletter to local craft and scrapbooking stores, clubs or groups. (Don't use the same content for different customers.) Build your own newsletter clientele. Create a whiz-bang issue and send a complimentary copy with subscription rates to potential clients and everyone you know who likes to scrapbook. Feature a new product or technique in each issue, suggest ideas for seasonal themes or provide a question-and-answer column. Describe new trends and report on conventions, expos and trade shows. Offer to write newsletters for other scrapbooking businesses. Make a pitch to your local scrapbook store to write their newsletter. Convince scrapbook product manufacturers that a newsletter can increase sales...and you're just the one to write it.

■ **Websites.** Scrapbook websites need product reviews, information about new products and trends, and articles about scrapping in general. Pay may be minimal or just a thank you. You may be paid with scrapbooking materials or product discounts rather than cash, but writing for websites is a good way to build your portfolio and establish a network that can lead to future jobs.

Three Ways to Warm Up

Banish writer's block with one of these surefire remedies:

1. Write a page or two starting with, "When I was six, our family
   _____," or "red reminds me of_____," or some other beginning.

2. Visualize what you're writing about. Lean back, close your eyes and
   see it before you put pen to paper.

3. Brainstorm about your topic and write down everything that comes to
   mind. Don't edit and organize your writing until your hand aches and
   you're out of ideas.

■ **Product manufacturers.** If you can write intriguing copy that makes scrappers want to rush out and buy new products, consider writing promotional material for scrapbooking manufacturers and distributors.

■ **Journaling for others.** If you have a penchant for poetry or a skill for storytelling, you can transform scrappers' memories and anecdotes into memorable album additions.

■ **Books**. Make a proposal to a publisher or publish your own work (see *Think Big with a Book* later in this chapter).

How to Sell Magazine Articles

Magazines have a specific process for accepting articles from freelance writers. Here are a few tips for mastering that process to get paid for your articles.

Know your market. Study several back issues of each publication before you pitch an idea. What format, length and style does the magazine favor? What topics have they included in past issues? Do articles typically include sidebars (boxes of information that run in the borders alongside an article)?

Has your idea already been covered by the magazine (don't bother suggesting the idea unless you have new or different information). Which articles are written by the staff and which are contributed by freelancers (check the magazine's masthead in the front of the publication)? For example, *Creating Keepsakes'* frequent product reviews are written by staff members, so pitching your own roundup of product reviews would probably be a waste of your time— and the editor's.

Request the guidelines. Get a copy of the magazine's writers' guidelines before you submit an idea. This document describes the type of

The Freelancer's Bible

Updated annually, *Writer's Market* acceptable topics, contact information, and general pay rates for hundreds of magazines. Check your library or see www.writersmarket.com. If you plan to write for magazines, invest in your own copy; it's money well spent.

articles the magazine wants, who to contact, pay rates, how to suggest topics, and whether the publisher prefers contact by e-mail or letter. To find the guidelines for a particular publication, check the publication's own website or request quidelines by sending a self-addressed stamped envelope (SASE) to the address listed on the magazine's masthead.

Write a query. Professional writers sell articles before writing them. Most magazines editors prefer to see a "query"—a one-page letter that describes your idea—instead of the finished article. Your query is what sells the story to the editor. If she can't use your idea, you haven't wasted time writing the story.

Magazine editors receive stacks of queries each week. Yours must stand out from the crowd. How do you do that? As a preview of your potential article, your query must be the very best example of your writing ability. First study the articles of the publication you're targeting. Note the type of information they provide, and the writing style. Then begin your query with a compelling opening that makes the editor want to read more. Tell why the publication's readers will benefit from your article and why you're the best one to write it. Mention whether you'll provide illustrations or sample pages. Rewrite and proof your query until it is perfect, then send it off to the editor with two or three clips that are representative of your best writing. Most magazines prepare issues four to six months ahead of the publication date, so send your seasonal queries in plenty of time.

There are lots of very good resources for learning about writing queries, including the books and writer's websites listed at the end of this chapter. *Writer's Digest* and *Writer* magazines often feature information about the mechanics of writing good query letters. Check your library, the bookstores and the Internet.

Write the article or try again. If your query is accepted, an editor will contact you with the amount of payment, length of the article, your deadline and a contract. Then it's time to sit down and deliver. If the magazine doesn't respond to your query in the time specified in their guidelines, give the editor a call or send an e-mail. If a rejection letter appears in your mailbox, don't despair! Send your query on to different publications or develop another idea and try again. All writers experience rejection—usually lots of it. It's part of the business. Continue to sharpen your writing skills, narrowly focus your ideas and develop query letters that editors just can't resist.

One day you'll receive a call, e-mail or letter from an editor welcoming your idea and promising a paycheck. Once you complete an article for a magazine, immediately follow up with another idea. Then, when you've written several pieces for the same editor, ask to become a regular contributor or propose your own column.

Write for Scrapbook Magazines

Scrapbook magazines are always looking for fresh ideas to interest readers. If you've mastered a special technique or created layouts you've never seen in scrapping magazines, you may have a writing assignment just around the corner. Maybe you have an idea for an informational and entertaining interview with a scrapping expert. Send your queries to the following scrapping magazines:

Creating Keepsakes. Send query to Editor-in-Chief Jana Lillie, 14901 Heritagecrest Way, Bluffdale, UT 84065 (www.creatingkeepsakes.com) or fax to (801) 765-9899.

Tips from a Pro

As Assistant Editor for *Creating Keepsakes,* Deanna Lambson writes for each issue and contributes to the magazine's editorial direction. Deanna offers these tips for freelancers:

1. Give yourself time to grow into your writing ability.

2. Decide what tone you want to take: nostalgic, lighthearted or reflective. How do you want people to feel when they read your article?

3. Try new approaches. For example, if you're used to writing in a technical way, practice something lighter.

4. Think before you write! Brainstorm and give your ideas time to blossom.

Memory Makers. Send query to Amy Partain, Copy Editor, 12365 Huron St., #500, Denver, CO 80345 or e-mail editorial@memorymakersmagazine.com.

Ivy Cottage Creations. Send query to Editor Pam Baird, P.O. Box 50688, Provo, Utah 84605 or e-mail support@ivycottagecreations.com.

PaperKuts. Send query or finished manuscript to Editor Kellene Adams, 232 West 540 North Holland Square, Orem, UT 84057, or e-mail editor@paperkuts.com.

Write Clearly, Simply, and Specifically

Choose your written words carefully:

- Check the dictionary to be sure you use words correctly. Use a thesaurus for alternative words with the same meaning.

- Don't use several words if one or two work just as well (or better); write "now" instead of "at this point in time."

- Be precise. Write "use a two-inch border of navy cardstock," instead of "use a blue border.."

Think Big with a Book

A career as an author depends on your ability to choose marketable topics and assess the competition, as well as your writing ability. Can your introduction to scrapping compete with the recognition and full-color layouts of *The Joy of Scrapbooking*? Can it compare to *The Idiot's Guide to Scrapbooking*?

Put on your thinking cap to consider topics for idea books. Write a show- and-tell about making borders with die-cuts and stickers, or publish a book of quotations, poems, page toppers or other writings for scrappers. How about a collection of time-saving techniques or tips from professional scrappers?

Consider the market: what do scrappers need that is not already available? Then write up a storm to provide a book scrappers just can't live without.

You can either sell your idea to a publisher or self-publish your work. The option involves a tradeoff: publishers take care of everything but the writing. They edit, typeset, print and distribute your book. Some will market your book, although you may be expected to do that too. Typically, you'll receive royalties of 4-10% of the cover price. You may also receive a small advance against those royalties. Find publishers in *Writer's Market* or check the front pages of scrapbooking books, then request their submission guidelines. Alternatively, you may want to hire an agent (who will retain 10-15% of your royalties) to peddle your book to publishers.

If you prefer to keep all the profits and don't mind sacrificing future writing time, you can self-publish your book. That means you do the writing, editing, illustrating, typesetting and marketing as well. You can also outsource many of these tasks. As a self-publisher, you make all the decisions about how your book will look and how it is priced. Most of your work, however, will involve marketing instead of writing. How much you make depends on how well you sell your book. You decide whether to sell to bookstores, scrapbooking stores or from your own website. Wholesale distributors will provide your book to their networks of bookstores (usually for a 55% discount). Your income depends primarily on how well you market your book.

The Art of Storytelling

When Janice Dixon's six children were small, she made each of them a treasured scrapbook. The books didn't have fancy layouts or many photos, but were filled with stories spun from Mom's special memories. Years later, Janice believed other scrappers would want to know how to transform their own children's actions and witticisms into stories. The result is her self-published guide, *The Art of Writing Scrapbook Stories.* Janice received permission from suppliers to use their products for page samples. Some even provided layouts. Contact Mt. Olympus Press (801) 486-3873 or www.aros.net/~discus/mop10.htm.

Make Time to Write

Many people say they just can't find the time to write. The truth is, we make time for things that are most important in our lives. When writing becomes a priority, you'll make time for it.

Write every day. Just like scrapping, good writing becomes easier and improves with practice, practice and more practice. The more you write, the more you improve. Try different techniques, methods and styles. Write about your day, your problems, your joys, your scrapping—everything and anything. It's also great therapy.

Nurture your writing and watch it grow. Keep a notebook by your bed and write a few pages before you go to sleep each night. It doesn't have to be epic work. Just write. Describe the delicate beauty of the tulips in the

Seven Tips to Improve Your Writing

1. READ! The best writers are voracious readers.

2. Organize your writing into manageable parts.

3. Give your writing a logical beginning, middle and end.

4. Be stingy. If a paragraph, word, or phrase doesn't add value, get rid of it.

5. Write your first draft without stopping to edit.

6. Let your writing "rest" for a few days. Then read it again, edit and rewrite.

7. Attend writing classes, take online tutorials and join writing groups to continually improve your writing.

front yard, how you feel when your child smiles, or how a particular political issue makes you want to scream.

Set a regular schedule. Are you a morning person? Do you perk up just when every one else is heading for bed? Decide when you're most creative and adjust your schedule accordingly to fit in some writing time. Be serious about the time you set aside and make the most of it.

Find a special place. Write where you'll be undisturbed. Try not to respond to distractions—the phone, your pager or messenger pigeons. If solitude isn't possible at home, head for the library, go to Starbuck's or hide in your favorite place to be alone.

Be prepared to write when ideas occur. Don't trust your memory when the perfect idea occurs to you. Carry a notebook or pad of paper with you and place an extra next to the bed. When the lightbulb in your head goes off, jot it down for future reference.

More Writer Resources

Books and Publications
- *This Business of Writing* by Gregg Levoy

- *The Elements of Style* by William Strunk Jr. and E.B. White

- *How To Write A Query Letter* by Lisa Collier Cool

- *The Writer's Guide to Query Letters & Cover Letters* by Gordon Burgett

- *How to Get Happily Published* by Judith Appelbaum

- *Guide to Literary Agents* edited by Rachel Vater

- *The Complete Guide to Self-Publishing* by Tom & Marilyn Ross

- *The Self-Publishing Manual* by Dan Poynter

- *The Writer's Guide to Self-Promotion and Publicity* by Elane Feldman

■ *1,001 Ways to Market Your Books* by John Kremer

■ *Writers Digest* magazine (800-333-0133 or see web reference below)

<u>On the Internet</u>
■ Visit these sites for tips, tutorials and information for writers: FreelanceWriting.com (www.freelancewriting.com), Writers (www.writers.com), Writer's Digest (www.writersdigest.com and www.writersonlineworkshops.com), and Inscriptions (www.inscriptionsmagazine.com). To find more sites devoted to writing, search the Internet using keywords "writer" and "writing"

■ Join a local writers' group. Check with bookstores or libraries in your area.

■ Check the course rosters at your local college or university for writing courses

Part III:
Understanding Business Basics

- ⊙ What It Means to Be a Professional
- ⊙ Should You Consider a Partner?
- ⊙ Start-Up Essentials
- ⊙ Critical Business Skills
- ⊙ Start-Up Checklists

If your head tells you one thing and your heart tells you another, before
you do anything, you should first decide whether you have a better head or
a better heart.—Marilyn Vos Savant

Chapter 13.
What It Means To
Be A Professional

As a business owner, you enter the realm of the professional. What,
exactly, does that mean? According to Webster's dictionary:

> pro•fes•sion•al: \pro-fesh-nal.
> *n.* one who engages in an occupation for financial return

To anyone who cares about their business, being professional means much more
than simply accepting payment for a service or product. Consider the following.

A Professional:
Apologizes for a customer's dissatisfaction
Builds lasting relationships
Communicates clearly
Delivers more than expected
Educates employees
Freely provides ideas
Gives solutions instead of excuses
Has patience with negative customers
Is proud of her business
Jumps to take advantage of opportunities

Keeps accurate and timely records
Listens and learns from customer complaints
Makes business fun
Names her business something clever and memorable
Offers help willingly
Pays bills on time
Quickly responds to customer inquiries
Refunds money with a smile
Shows employees they're appreciated
Treats everyone courteously
Uniquely competes in the market
Values honesty
Weighs the advantages and disadvantages of decisions
X-rays the competition
Yields when appropriate
Zealously pursues her business

Is the Customer Always Right?

It's an unfortunate fact of doing business: a few customers go out of their way to stretch "the customer is always right" philosophy. You may encounter customers who buy your paper-piecing patterns long enough to trace them and then return them for a refund. Or customers who constantly come into your store for free advice and never make a purchase. There are buyers who are always dissatisfied with something... but keep making purchases and then returning them. Having patience and giving customers the benefit of the doubt is just part of doing business—but it doesn't mean you have to let a few sour grapes step all over you or curse your employees. If you refuse a customer's request, remain professional. Often a calm demeanor and a logical explanation will do the trick.

Opportunities are usually disguised by hard work, so most people don't recognize them.—Ann Landers

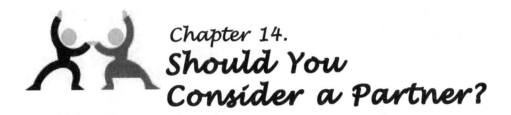

Chapter 14.
Should You Consider a Partner?

Working by yourself means you wear all the hats: you have all the responsbility, make all the decisions and keep all the profits. If you're willing to share all that, a partner can be a refreshing source of ideas, skills and energy—if you choose the right person. You can describe the ups and downs of your business with friends or family, but no one can commiserate like a partner who is equally committed. Having a partner means you can divide responsibilities and focus on your part of the business, instead of trying to handle everything yourself.

Not Just Any Old Partner Will Do

Because of the complex interpersonal relationships involved, choosing a business partner may be one of the most important decision you'll ever make. Your partnership is a business marriage—a partner can make or break you. If you've ever been in a friendship gone awry or a bad relationship, you can imagine how disastrous that kind of problem would be in a business.

Sharing a passion for scrapbooking isn't enough reason to pick a partner. At the very least, your partner should be someone who shares your enthusiasm and business goals. Choose someone who complements your expertise *and* personality—someone who'll share the load, not add to it.

Maybe you're a fabulous scrapper with no business skills, and your partner is a former retail whiz. Perhaps you're more of a "people" person than a number cruncher and your partner loves details and budgets. The two of you don't always have to agree on everything (although that would be nice), but you must be able to make decisions together without frequent disagreements, ill will or hurt feelings. Two heads *are* better than one, especially when you both view your business with gusto and work toward the same goals.

How 'Bout Cousin Clem?

Thinking of a friend or family member as your partner? Before offering a partnership, consider whether they would be a business blessing or a bull in a china shop. If you don't get along well outside the business, odds are you, and your customers, will have the same experience inside.

Put It in Writing

If you're going to have a partner (or partners), *always* start with a written agreement. You never know what will happen down the line. A written agreement ensures a mutual understanding and acceptance of how you'll make decisions, share repsonsibilities and split profits. At the very least, your partnership agreement should clearly address the following ittems:

■ Your business goals.

■ The responsibilities of each partner.

■ The financial contributions of each partner.

■ How profits and losses will be shared.

■ How decisions will be made.

■ How conflicts or disagreements will be resolved.

■ What happens if a partner dies or decides to discontinue the relationship.

Survey Says!

- Partners in scrapbook retail stores
  Spouse: 33%
  Family member: 33%
  Friend: 33%

Is Your Spouse a Good Choice?

What happens when you mix marriage and business? Many couples say the required dependency, trust and teamwork strengthens their relationship. Sharing a business can be a blissful opportunity—or way too much togetherness. Running a business is stressful and demanding. If you have difficulty communicating with your spouse or your best never seems to be good enough, think twice before the two of you launch a professional joint venture.

Working together may also be a strain on the family. Which of you will get the kids ready for school or take them to soccer practice? If you don't compromise on family issues, how will you make business decisions together? Do some serious soul searching before you decide to work together.

Profile: Nancy and Dale Bohrer

Nancy Bohrer, owner of Dream Events, Inc., comments on operating her business with husband Dale: "For years I dreamed of starting my own business. Nothing worked well enough to allow my husband to work with me, until scrapbooking came into our lives. For us, working side by side is a dream come true, hence the name of our business. We talk about things that interest both of us. When there's a problem I go to the one who knows me best—my partner in love, life and business. And when everything is going good, we can enjoy our success together. It is really the best way to live."

Seven Tips for Working with Your Spouse (Without Losing Your Mind)

1. Respect each other.

2. Keep your sense of humor.

3. Share the same goals.

4. Decide how you'll split responsibilities.

5. Keep the lines of communication open.

6. Make time for individual pursuits and "together time" away from the business.

7. Never go to sleep angry.

More Partner Resources

Books

- *Finding Your Perfect Soulmate or Business Partner* by David E. Smith, Jr. and Bernard Adolphus

- *The Partnership Maker* and *The Partnership Book* by Denis Clifford and Ralph Warner

The way I see it, if you want the rainbow, you gotta be willing to put up with the rain.—Dolly Parton

Chapter 15.
Start-up Essentials

Now that you've thought about what you want from a business and which pursuit best fits your personal and professional goals, it's time to review a few business fundamentals. This section is by no means everything you'll need, but it will give you a glimpse into what's required before you begin.

Establish Your Legal Structure

One of the first decisions you'll make is how to legally structure your business. Your decision may have legal implications and requirements, and will determine how you'll file tax returns. For just $10, you can log on to Nolo Press' website at www.nolopress.com and download *"Choosing a Structure for Your Small Business."*

Sole Proprietorship. This is the easiest, most common and least expensive legal business structure. If you don't incorporate your business or form a legal partnership, the IRS will, by default, consider you a sole proprietor.

As a sole proprietor, you have all the responsibility and keep all the profits. You also pay all the bills and are *personally* responsible for any business debts you incur. This means a disgruntled customer who falls in your store or an unpaid vendor can sue for your personal and business assets.

Your business taxes are filed on Schedule C along with your personal return.

Partnership. If you have one or more business partners and you don't incorporate, your business is automatically considered a partnership. Legally, partners can be held personally responsible for each other's business debts.

If an investor has a financial stake in your business, but won't be involved in the day-to-day-operations or decision-making, your structure is a limited partnership and may need to be registered with your county or state. You operate the business as if you were a sole proprietor, while your investors' liabilities are limited to the amount of their investments. The partnership itself pays no taxes. Individual partners pay income tax on their shares of the profits. If you plan to operate your business with your spouse, you may still operate as a sole proprietorship, with one of you designated as the official owner of the business.

Corporation. If you plan to become a retail store owner, event planner or product designer, you may want to consider forming a corporation. Why? Because as a corporation, your personal assets are usually protected from any lawsuits filed against your business.

Contrary to popular myth, forming a corporation does not automatically entitle you to a lower tax rate. But it does require you to generate specific reports and form a Board of Directors (which could be you, your mom and your sister). See a lawyer regarding your state's incorporation rules and potential liability.

Play the Name Game

Choose a memorable and descriptive business name. Which is more appealing: "Mary Jane Mazerowkowski's Scrapbooks" or "Down Memory Lane?"

One creative method for choosing a clever business name is to make two lists of words associated with your business: one list of nouns and the other list of verbs. Then combine different elements from both lists until you come up with a name you like. Hopefully, you'll be in business for a long time, so choose a name that will be meaningful as your business grows to provide additional products and services. If you're going to have a logo, design one with the same long-term characteristics.

The scope of the business you choose determines the extent to which you must register your business:

Local. Search county records to determine whether your business name is available. If it is, file a Ficticious Name Statement, also known as a DBA ("Doing Business As"), with the county. If your choice is already taken, select another name. Or contact the registered owner of the name to see if his business is still operating. If it isn't, he may be willing to file an Abandonment of Fictitious Name Statement, so you can register the name for your own use. Be careful about assuming a name associated with a business with a poor reputation or bad credit record.

In some states, if your business carries your first and last name, e.g., "Megan Magruder's Scrapbooks," you may not be required to file at all. Check with your county clerk's office.

State. Check state records to make sure another business within the state isn't already using the same business name. Contact your Secretary of State's office for a database search. If the name is available, register it to gain exclusive use of that name throughout your state.

National. You may not legally use a name that is trademarked by another business. Conduct a trademark search as described in Chapter 11. Refer to Chapter 6 for information about choosing business names for Internet websites.

Get Required Permits and Licenses

Business license requirements vary from county to county and state to state. Contact the appropriate agencies to determine what you need to do.

Local Business License. Check with your city clerk to determine whether you need a license to operate a business. You probably do and will need to pay a small annual fee.

Resale Permit. If your state collects sales tax, you'll need to apply for a resale permit with the State Board of Equalization or Department of Revenue. The permit is required to do business. It also exempts the sales tax on retail materials you buy and use to create products which you then sell.

If you create custom scrapbooks for example, any albums, papers or other items used in those scrapbooks are exempt from sales tax if you purchase them from a retail merchant. (Materials you buy from wholesalers is also exempt from sales tax.) When you sell your product to customers within your state, you must then collect the deferred sales tax. You'll be required to file reports quarterly or annually, depending on your business' annual income, to the appropriate agency, along with the sales taxes you've collected on behalf of the state.

Find Funding

How much money you need depends on the type of business you're starting, and the scale on which you intend to operate. Many scrappers fund their businesses with their savings, family loans or personal credit cards. Some sell off a car, boat, cabin or use an inheritance. Others split start-up and operating costs with a partner or investor.

If you find yourself shopping for a lender, your bank may seem like the logical place to start. Local banks, however, are often reluctant to give money to first-time businesses (they'll probably tell you to use your personal credit cards), particularly a crafts business (that's how they see scrapbooking). Other possibilities include taking a loan on your life insurance (the interest rate is usually lower than bank loans) or your 401(k) retirement plan. If you fill out a brief application at LiveCapital.com (www.livecapital.com), the site will quickly return a list of potential lenders, their fees and interest rates. You may also qualify for an SBA-guaranteed loan (if you're turned down three or more times by a bank), or an SBA Micro Loan up to $25,000. Be ready to prove your case with a well-documented business plan before you approach a lender.

Open a Business Checking Account

Be ready when your profits start rolling in. Take your DBA and resale permit to your bank and open a business checking account. Take the time to separate your personal and business funds, something the IRS looks for when it determines whether your business is really a hobby. Checking account fees and services are competitive. Shop around for the best deal you can find. Check to see whether your bank requires a minimum monthly balance and if you can access your account online.

Establish a Merchant Account

If you're operating a small local business and your customers pay you by cash or check, you may not need to accept credit cards. Accepting credit cards is a must, however, for retail and Internet stores. Establish a merchant account to authorize and process customer credit card payments. Don't settle for just any merchant account; plenty of card processing companies want your business. Shop around for competitive rates. Search the Internet using the keywords "merchant account" to compare fees, transaction rates and service requirements.

Here's how the process works: Once you have a merchant account, you can process customer credit card orders either manually (swiping the card with a small terminal) or electronically (using your computer, modem and special software). The latter method connects you with the card processing company's database which provides almost instant verification. The payment is deposited into your bank account within 48 hours, minus a small fee (usually two to five percent of the total, depending on the type of business you operate and your transaction volume). Some companies charge more for Internet and homebased businesses.

Create Promotional Materials

Once you've decided on a name for your business, have business cards made with your contact information and logo. Hire a printer or use your computer to print your own materials. Another alternative is to develop your own design and have your local copy shop print the materials for you. There are also many discount printing companies on the Internet, like iPrint.com (www.iprint.com), Vista Print (www.vistaprint.com) and others, who regularly offer an initial order of business cards at no charge.

Order or create business letterhead, envelopes and promotional brochures. Don't forget to create something special to announce your grand opening. If you'll be shipping products, you'll also need mailing labels. Order custom labels from a local or Internet printing company. Or simply buy blank computer labels at an office supply store, then copy and paste your company logo and return address. Address by hand or with your computer.

Check Office Max, Office Depot or your local office supply store or contact Viking Supplies at (800) 421-1222 (www.vikingop.com) for a copy of their catalog. Viking has very competitive prices and delivers to your home or business within 24 hours of receiving your order.

Insure Your Business

Depending on the type of business you choose, your investment and potential financial liability, you may want to obtain business insurance. Consider coverage for fire, flood, theft and liability, particularly if you're planning to open a retail store. Weigh the pros and cons of additional insurance for a home store or other scrapbook businesses.

If you're going to plan crops, conventions, expos, getaways or other functions, check to see what liability insurance is carried by the event facility, and what additional coverage you may need to obtain.

Obtain Employer Information

As an employer, you're subject to more rules and regulations than a sole proprietor. If you're going to hire employees, apply for the following:

■ An Employer Identification Number (EIN) is used to identify your business on tax returns and licenses. Partnerships and corporations must use EINs, while sole proprietors may use their social security numbers or file for an EIN. Contact the IRS for Form SS-4.

■ Become familiar with your state's requirements for operating a business. Most states require employers to withhold state income tax from employee's paychecks, contribute to unemployment insurance and pay Worker's Compensation Insurance. *The Employer's Tax Guide* (IRS Publication #15) includes federal withholding tables and W-4 forms for your employees. Contact the IRS for more information. See Chapter 16 for more information about taxes.

■ All employers must comply with the Occupational Safety & Health Administration (OSHA) regulations, minimum wage and overtime payments and other Department of Labor regulations. Contact (202) 693-4650, see www.dol.gov, or visit your nearest regional office for details.

More Start-Up Essentials Resources

Books and Publications
■ *Complete Idiot's Guide to Starting Your Own Business* by Ed Paulson

■ *The Small Business Start-Up Guide* by Robert Sullivan

■ *Small Time Operator* by Bernard Kamoroff, CPA

On the Internet
■ Find lots of helpful information, inspiration and ideas at Quicken.com (www.quicken.com), Small Business Advisor (www.isquare.com), and the Small Business Administration (www.sba.gov). You can find many more resources online by searching for key word "Small Business"

If you can't do it excellently don't do it at all. Because if it's not excellent it won't be profitable or fun, and if you're not in business for fun or profit, what are you doing here?—Robert Townsend, *Up the Organization*

Chapter 16.
Critical Business Skills

By now, you know scrapreneurs wear many hats—planner, stock clerk, sales representative, even janitor—to keep their businesses humming along successfully. This chapter introduces some of the additional skills that are crucial to business success.

Develop a Business Plan

Many small business owners dread the thought of putting a business plan together, but it's an incredibly helpful planning tool. It's a must if you're going to pursue financing from a bank or investors, who will want to see the potential of your business before lending you money. Whether your business is small or large, part-time or full-time, developing a business plan before you begin is the singlemost important planning activity you can undertake. It's professional suicide to start a significant undertaking—like a retail store or product development—without one.

A business plan helps to organize and clarify your thinking and identifies areas needing additional research and planning. Quality, not quantity, counts here. Your business plan needn't be several inches thick, but should be prepared carefully and thoughtfully. Your plan is the roadmap for your path to success: you may not be able to find your way without it.

Create your start-up business plan with projections and information from your planning and research. Once you've been in business for a while, update your plan based on your experience. It will be well worth your while to attend a business plan workshop (contact the SBA, SCORE, business incubators, or your local college). There are also many helpful books, magazines and websites. Business plan software, like Business Plan Pro at (800) 229-7526 or www.businessplanpro.com, prompts you for information, then automatically formats your plan. Another resource, Bplans.com, has examples of sample business plans.

Business plans can be created in different ways. Your conclusions are far more important than format. Generally, however, your business plan should include the following segments:

Introduction. Develop your cover page, table of contents and an executive summary. These key pieces of your business plan come in handy if you're courting lenders.

Business description. Describe the healthy business potential in the scrapbooking industry, your products and services and how you intend to succeed in the marketplace. Discuss your pricing strategies.

Market analysis. Define your target market and growth potential. Assess your competition: who are they, where are they, what are their strengths and weaknesses and how will you compete with them.

Operations. Tell how you'll start your business, including implementation, location, labor requirements and how you'll find suppliers. Describe the day-to-day business operations, including hours of operation, how your business will be managed and staffing plans (number of employees, their responsibilities, benefits and training plans).

Sales and marketing. State your plans for promoting your business. Tell how you will find customers. Identify distribution channels, suppliers, type, cost and frequency of advertising and promotion.

Management. Name the owners and the qualifications they bring to the business (or include their resumés). If you're incorporated, identify your Board of Directors, how often it will meet and how it will function.

Financial projections. Provide a summary of startup costs. Describe your financial risk. Develop a cash flow analysis and balance sheet. Provide a monthly budget for your first year of operation, a profit-and-loss projection for the first year or two and schedule your breakeven point. (These terms are defined below.)

Explain how you'll make up for less-than-expected profits. List your salary and employee wages. Explain growth plans and how profits will be reinvested. State the types of payments you'll accept and how they will be processed. Define the accounting method you'll use.

Get Acquainted With Finance Fundamentals

Mention "budget" or "accounting" and many entrepreneurs run screaming from the room. Accounting terminology is less intimidating if you take the time to master a few financial basics. Don't leave your professional destiny to chance: actively manage your business finances to avoid costly surprises at the end of the month.

Here's why financial skills are so important to your business:

■ They provide guidelines for operating within your budget.

■ They keep you on track toward your financial goals.

■ They determine whether your business is profitable.

■ They provide information for required reporting (sales tax, business tax, personal tax and corporate reports).

The following financial items are fundamental to your business.

1. **Start-up costs**. Use the following formula to estimate the cost of starting your business:

> One-time start-up expenses[1]
> + Estimated monthly expenses[2]
> + Amount of contingency fund[3]
> = Total start-up investment

[1]The costs required to get your business started. Checklist #2 in Chapter 17 will help you track these costs by activity and item.

[2]The amount needed to keep your business running until it starts paying for itself (monthly operational cost times the number of months until you realize your projected profit). Note: If you're depending on your business income to cover personal living expenses, include those in this total too. Use Checklist #3 in Chapter 17.

[3]This "stash" is used to offset unexpected expenses, slower-than-expected profits and other unforeseen costs.

2. **Breakeven analysis.** This analysis shows how much money you need to repay the cost of doing business. Any additional income is profit.

3. **Cash flow analysis.** This document accounts for money flowing in and out of your business. It's one of the most important business reports because it reflects the financial state of your business at any given time.

4. **Balance sheet**. This is a snapshot of how well your business is doing on any given day. It's a summary of your assets (what your business owns), liabilities (what your business owes) and net worth (the difference between your assets and liabilities).

5. **Profit-and-loss statement.** This document uses data from the cash flow analysis and balance sheet to determine whether you're making a profit.

In addition to these skills, strive to follow sound financial strategies:

■ Set financial goals. Whether you work 10 or 60 hours a week at your business, set specific goals to help achieve the profit you want.

■ Learn to operate on a budget. Monitor purchases to stay within your spending boundaries.

■ Learn retail finance. General business skills are important no matter what scrapbooking endeavor you choose. A retail operation, however, involves unique financial issues such as margins, inventory turns, and other complexities. Take a course on retail finance if you plan to start a homebased, Internet or traditional retail store.

■ Consult a professional when necessary. Hire an accountant and/or a lawyer to help navigate complex tax laws, set up your corporate books and explain equipment depreciation and amortization.

■ Reinvest in your business. If possible, use a portion of your profits to enhance your services or promote your business.

Keep Accurate Records

Can you imagine the result of continually writing checks without making entries in your checkbook? How would you know when you're overdrawn? That's exactly why you need to maintain accurate business records. Trying to work backwards to figure out what you've spent, what you owe and what you've taken in is a frustrating, time-consuming task. Whether you're using a

Keep 'Em Straight

If you have more than one business, maintain a complete and separate set of records for each business. Keep all business records separate from your personal records.

handwritten ledger, a spreadsheet or a POS, establish recordkeeping from the start. Be judicious about keeping your accounts current. Here are a few benefits of keeping accurate records:

■ **Monitoring the progress of your business**. Good records reflect which products are selling and which are not, how your money is spent, whether your business is improving and whether you're making a profit.

■ **Providing accurate tax return data.** Recordkeeping provides information required for state and federal income tax returns and filing your state sales tax reports. It also supports your tax deductions. If you're audited, you can't support what isn't properly recorded.

■ **Proving your business isn't a hobby.** If you don't show a profit in three of the last five years, the IRS may decide your business is really a hobby and negate your previous business expense deductions unless your records show you do try to make a profit. Be cautious about what you write off as a deduction and what you don't. While you may never be audited, be sure you can truly connect every deductible expense to your business.

Make It Easy

The key to good recordkeeping is accuracy and consistency. A computer spreadsheet or a handwritten ledger from the stationary store may be fine for your small business. For a business with a large inventory or complex financials, use QuickBooks, QuickBooks Pro, Peachtree First Accounting, a POS system or other recordkeeping software. Be consistent about entering transactions and keeping your database current.

Make Sense of Regulations and Red Tape

You'll keep government agencies happy and simplify your business life by complying with regulations and paying your share of taxes. Here's an idea of what you'll encounter:

■ **State sales tax.** As described in Chapter 15, you're required to remit sales tax collected to the state in which you live.

■ **Estimated income tax.** Business taxes are filed with your personal income tax return. You may be required to estimate business taxes quarterly if your annual income is $500 or more.

■ **Employer and employee taxes.** As an employer, you're responsible for paying additional taxes and withholding certain taxes from employees' paychecks, as shown on the next page.

Type of Tax	Employee Contribution	Company Contribution
State income tax	Yes	No
Federal income tax	Yes	No
Social Security	Yes	Yes
Medicare	Yes	Yes
Federal Unemployment	No	Yes
State Unemployment	No	Depends on the state

■ **Business tax deductions.** Good news! You're allowed to deduct the cost of doing business from your income tax. The money you spend on inventory, advertising, shipping, leasing space, your salary, employee wages and benefits, building and maintaining your website, subscriptions to scrapbooking magazines, the cost of attending scrapbooking events and other business expenses are generally deductible. You may also depreciate equipment purchased for your business, including computer hardware, die-cut machines, store cabinets, display fixtures and furniture. Mileage driven for business purposes is also deductible. (Your total deductions can't exceed your profit.)

Unless your business is incorporated, you can also deduct the portion of your home used *exclusively* for business. The area or room can't be used for any other purpose. You can't, for example, deduct your bedroom just because you work from a desk there and store inventory in a box under the bed. Nor can you deduct a home office if your primary business location is your retail store—even if you do some work at home.

Save for Those Twilight Years

If you can afford to set aside a portion of your earnings each year, you can take advantage of one of the best tax shelters available to the self-employed: funding your own retirement plan. Check with the IRS or ask your accountant about a Simplified Employee Pension Plan and a Keough Plan.

Promote Your Business

Know who your customers are and what they want. Actively promote your business. Follow your marketing plan. Each month, think of new ways to find new customers, sell more products and provide additional services. Generously hand out business cards.

Build a strong support network. Look for ways to share ideas, frustrations and successes with others in the scrapbook industry. Your competitors may not invite you over for coffee and scones, but many business owners in the industry go out of their way to help each other.

Talk to other retailers and consultants at conventions and expos. Join e-mail groups listed throughout this book. Get involved in your community and local Chamber of Commerce. Use expos, conventions, and trade shows to your advantage. Be proud of your business. Take every opportunity to tell people what you do.

Learn from Your Mistakes

If we stopped doing something every time we encountered failure, we'd never get anywhere! Babies don't stop trying to walk each time they fall down. You don't stop creating layouts because your first border was lopsided. It's the same with business—it's a learning experience. Realize that you will make mistakes. If you've prepared well, your boo boos will be of the small fry variety rather than something with dreadful impact. Don't think of your mistakes as failures. Consider them as ways to acquire new knowledge and skills that will help your business grow and thrive. It helps to know as much as you can before you begin, but you can't know everything.

Find Help When You Need It

When an aspect of your business gets you down or blocks your progress, don't be shy about asking for help. Spend some time in the library, chat with a SCORE representative, or speak with fellow scrapreneur. Take action before problems get out of hand. Deal with stress, frustration and exhaustion. Find ways to stay motivated and positive about your business.

More Critical Skills Resources

Books and Publications

■ *Bookkeeping On Your Home-Based PC* by Linda Stern

■ *Guerrilla Marketing: Secrets for Making Big Profits from Small Business* by Jay Levinson

■ *How to Write a Business Plan* by Mike McKeever

■ *Tax Savvy* for Small Businesses by Fred W. Daily

■ *Business Start-Ups* and *Entrepreneur* magazines (800 274-6229)

■ The IRS has a variety of helpful publications for small businesses. Request *Your Business Tax Kit* (an assortment of forms and publications to help business owners), *Guide to Free Tax Services, Small Business Tax Education Program,* and *Tax Rules for HB Biz* (Pub 587). Contact your local IRS office or call (800) 829-3676 for these publications and many others (see the IRS reference below)

On the Internet

■ Find information, questions and answers, ideas, and tips about business plans at the SBA's website (www.sba.gov/starting/businessplan.html) and the Business Know-how website (www.businessknowhow.com). Search for key words "business plan" for additional helpful sites

■ Use Katsuey's Legal Gateway (www.katsuey.com) For help with legal issues or use Nolo Press' (www.nolo.com) online legal encyclopedia and "Ask Auntie Nolo." Nolo also has several books on various legal issues which may be purchased or downloaded from the website

■ Find answers to your tax questions and download tax forms at the IRS website (www.irs.gov)

All good decisions in life are based on research. If you're smart enough to research what you're doing, you can make better decisions.—Warren Avis, founder of Avis Car Rental

Chapter 17.
Start-up Checklists

There's no doubt about it. Starting a business can be overwhelming. There's so much to consider, so much to plan, and so much to get done before you conduct your first transaction. Just thinking about all the weeks or months of "getting ready" activities can make your head spin. Approaching your business carefully and thoughtfully, taking it one step at a time, will eliminate much of the confusion. Good planning can also remove much of the guesswork and potential nasty surprises that may await down the road. The more you know beforehand, the better prepared you'll be.

One of the most common start-up mistakes is underestimating the cost of beginning and maintaining a business. Believe it or not, in their zeal to get their businesses going (and rake in tons of money), many people skip as many planning steps as they can. They usually pay for it later.

The start-up checklists in this chapter will help you identify both activities and costs. (You don't need to complete activities in the order shown.) Some items, such as "define personal and business goals," may not cost you anything; however if you take a workshop, buy a book or pay a professional to help you create that list, you would include that cost. Delete and add items as applicable to your business. When you're finished, you'll have a good idea of what it will cost to begin and operate your business.

Checklist #1: Estimated Start-Up Activities and Costs

__Activities__   __Cost__

Planning
❏ Create Fear List and Action Steps
❏ Define personal and business goals   _____
❏ Decide which business is right for you   _____
❏ Research requirements for business selected   _____
❏ Develop knowledge/skills inventory   _____
❏ Assess financial resources   _____
❏ Attend small business course or seminar   _____
❏ Conduct market research   _____
❏ Assess competition and financial risk   _____
❏ Create marketing plan/business plan   _____
❏ Schedule start-up date   _____
❏ _____   _____
❏ _____   _____
❏ _____   _____
❏ _____   _____
Planning Subtotal $_____

Business Infrastructure
❏ Determine legal structure
❏ Register business name/file DBA   _____
❏ Check zoning laws   _____
❏ Obtain city/county business license(s)   _____
❏ Obtain state sales permit/license(s)   _____
❏ Retain lawyer   _____
❏ Hire consultant   _____
❏ Hire other professional (s)   _____
❏ File partnership or corporate documents   _____
❏ Request state/federal tax forms/information   _____
❏ _____   _____
❏ _____   _____
Business Infrastructure Subtotal $_____

Activities   <u>Cost</u>

Setting Up Your Business

❑ Conduct copyright search   _____

❑ Register copyright   _____

❑ Conduct trademark search   _____

❑ Register trademark   _____

❑ Conduct patent search   _____

❑ Apply for patent   _____

❑ Open business checking account   _____

❑ Apply for business credit card   _____

❑ Establish merchant account   _____

❑ Order utilities telecommunications   _____

❑ Order telecommunications   _____

❑ Set up office and/or workspace   _____

❑ Buy office supplies   _____

❑ Establish accounting/recordkeeping/inventory systems   _____

❑ Establish website and e-mail   _____

❑ Create promotional materials   _____

❑ Develop advertising   _____

❑ Obtain insurance   _____

❑ Have cash on hand   _____

❑ Announce/advertise business opening   _____

❑ _____   _____

❑ _____   _____

❑ _____   _____

❑ _____   _____

Setting Up Your Business Subtotal $_____

Activities   **Cost**

Additional Activities for Retailers
❏ Attend a retail seminar
❏ Find a storefront   _____
❏ Buy existing business/franchise   _____
❏ Remodel/renovate/decorate   _____
❏ Sign lease; pay rent or lease deposit   _____
❏ Order fixtures and furniture   _____
❏ Order public utilities   _____
❏ Order telecommunications   _____
❏ Contact suppliers   _____
❏ Establish POS system   _____
❏ Set up accounting/recordkeeping systems   _____
❏ Order starting inventory   _____
❏ Price and stock inventory   _____
❏ Establish distribution channel   _____
❏ Order signage   _____
❏ _____   _____
❏ _____   _____
❏ _____   _____
❏ _____   _____
Additional Activities for Retailers Subtotal $_____

<u>Activities</u>   **<u>Cost</u>**

Additional Activities for Employers
❐ Contact Dept. of Labor to determine requirements   _____
❐ Contact IRS for employer tax requirements   _____
❐ Obtain state/federal employer identification numbers   _____
❐ Contact state labor department for worker's   _____
   compensation and other requirements
❐ Establish wage and benefit schedules   _____
❐ Hire and train employees   _____
❐ _____   _____
❐ _____   _____
❐ _____   _____
❐ _____   _____
Additional Activities for Employers Subtotal $_____

Planning Subtotal   _____
Business Infrastructure Subtotal   _____
Setting Up Your Business Subtotal   _____
Additional Activities for Retailers Subtotal   _____
Additional Activities for Employers Subtotal   _____
Total Estimated Start-up Costs $_____

Checklist #2: Estimated Monthly Expenses

Activities	Cost
❏ Advertising	_____
❏ Insurance	_____
❏ Inventory	_____
❏ Loan payment/interest	_____
❏ Maintenance	_____
❏ Legal/consulting/professional fees	_____
❏ Rent/lease	_____
❏ Shipping	_____
❏ Supplies	_____
❏ Utilities	_____
❏ Website maintenance/e-mail	_____
❏ Salary and wages	_____
❏ Payroll taxes	_____
❏ State taxes	_____
❏ Income taxes	_____
❏ Employer taxes	_____
❏ Other taxes	_____
❏ Health, dental and vision plan costs	_____
❏ _____	_____
❏ _____	_____
❏ _____	_____
❏ _____	_____

Total Estimated Monthly Expenses $_____

Note: Once you start your business, you can update this list with your actual numbers to provide a more accurate forecast of your monthly expenses.

Index

A

B

C

D

Carlo Press Publications

Tollfree Tel: (800) 431-1579
Fax: (650) 592-3790
Online: www.carlopress.com
E-mail: carlop@pacbell.net
U.S. mail: PO Box 7019, San Carlos, CA 94070

The Scrapbooker's Guide to Business:
What You Need to Know *Before* You Invest $14.95
Wondering how you can turn your scrapbooking passion into
a profitable business? Find out what you need to get started
in nine different part-time and full-time businesses.

Meals and Memories:
How To Create Keepsake Cookbooks $15.95
The only comprehensive guide for using scrapbooking tools
and techniques to create unforgettable recipe pages and
cookbook memory albums.

All books are shipped USPS Priority Mail unless other specified. We also
add state sales tax to all California orders.

Contact us for our wholesale terms.